GLOUCESTERSHI

Headquarters: SHIRE HA
Tel. Glou

This book should be retur
stamped below, but may b
another reader, by giving the
stamped.

BINGHAM LIBRA.   ...ENCESTER.
TEL: 3502 69813
MON. 10-5, TUES. 10-7, WED. 10-l,
THURS. & FRI. 10-7, SAT. 9.30-1.

CL.16   PD/L—3

1/84			19. FEB. 1986
18. FEB. 1984	21. SEP. 1984	-6. JUN. 1985	
14. MAR 1984	13. OCT. 1984		15. MAR. 1986
-7. APR. 1984		14. AUG. 1985	
27. APR. 1984	-4. DEC. 1984	30. SEP. 1985	-3. APR. 1986
	28. DEC. 1984		-7. MAY 1986
-4. JUN. 1984	11. FEB. 1985	26. NOV. 1985	
22. JUN. 1984	28. MAR 1985		
13. JUL 1984	23. APR. 1985	28. DEC. 1985	
	20. MAY 1985	11. JAN 1986	
17. AUG. 1984		10 FEB. 1986	
21. AUG. 1984			

Macmillan Computing Books

Assembly Language Programming for the BBC Microcomputer
Ian Birnbaum

Advanced Programming for the 16K ZX81   Mike Costello

Microprocessors and Microcomputers — their use and programming   Eric Huggins

The Alien, Numbereater, and Other Programs for Personal Computers – with notes on how they were written   John Race

Beginning BASIC   Peter Gosling

Continuing BASIC   Peter Gosling

Program Your Microcomputer in BASIC   Peter Gosling

Practical BASIC Programming   Peter Gosling

The Sinclair ZX 81 – Programming for Real Applications
Randle Hurley

More Real Applications for the Spectrum and ZX81   Randle Hurley

Assembly Language Assembled – for the Sinclair ZX81   Tony Woods

Digital Techniques   Noel Morris

Microprocessor and Microcomputer Technology   Noel Morris

Understanding Microprocessors   B. S. Walker

Codes for Computers and Microprocessors   P. Gosling and
Q. Laarhoven

Z80 Assembly Language Programming for Students   Roger Hutty

Practical BASIC Programming

P.E. Gosling
Formerly Principal Lecturer in Computing
Peterborough Technical College

© P.E. Gosling 1982

All rights reserved. No part of this publication may be reproduced or transmitted, in any form or by any means, without permission.

First published 1983 by
THE MACMILLAN PRESS LTD
London and Basingstoke
Companies and representatives
throughout the world

Printed in Hong Kong

ISBN 0 333 34591 6

The paperback edition of the book is sold subject to the condition that it shall not, by way of trade or otherwise, be lent, resold, hired out, or otherwise circulated without the publisher's prior consent in any form of binding or cover other than that in which it is published and without a similar condition including this condition being imposed on the subsequent purchaser.

Contents

Preface	vi
1. The BASIC language	1
2. Seeking out errors	12
3. Some simple programming problems	32
4. Real life problems	53
5. Using random access files	93

Preface

This book is designed to give practice in the writing of good, useful programs in BASIC. While there are all kinds of criticisms aimed at BASIC as a programming language it remains the most popular method for introducing new programmers to the science, or art, of programming. With all its failings BASIC is a very easy language to learn and use and once the rudiments have been mastered then some very sophisticated programs can be written. The object of this book is to present a number of practical problems together with suggestions as to how they might be solved. In addition a number of the obvious pitfalls are highlighted in Chapter 2. It is easy to write programs, but to write programs which work well and efficiently is another matter; not only that but the programmer must know how to test his program and what to do if something, as it always does, goes wrong. All the listed programs and files are available separately on a 5 1/4 inch flexidisc.

A number of programs and examples used in this text are based on problems published by the Open University as part of their PM951 "Computing and Computers" course. My grateful thanks is offered to the Open University for their permission to use the material which is taken from Assignments 5/1978, 4/1979, 4/1980, 5/1981 and 3a/1981 and from examination papers PM951/SP,PM951/I 1975, PM951/M 1976,PM951/H 1977 and PM951/H 1981.

The text for this book was produced on an ACT Sirius 1 microcomputer using the Wordstar (TM) word processing package and printed on a TEC Starwriter daisy wheel printer.

P.E.GOSLING

1. The BASIC language

Before commencing the programming exercises which make up the majority of this book we must first define the language we are going to use. BASIC, in common with all computer languages, exists in a number of dialects and it is only in the case of very simple programs that one written for one computer will run without modification on another. The generally accepted "standard" form of BASIC is known as Microsoft (TM) and it is around this version of the language that these programming examples are designed. BASIC consists of a number of "reserved" keywords and symbols. These are bound together in a formal structure of statements which are always preceded by a number known as a "line number".

nnnnn BASIC statement

A statement, or BASIC instruction, can be one of a series of types:

(1) A statement to input data into the computer's memory.

(2) A statement to output data from the computer's memory.

(3) A statement causing a "jump" to another part of the program – either conditionally or unconditionally.

(3) A statement causing an operation to be performed on the contents of memory.

(5) A non-executable statement such as REM or DIM.

The contents of memory are referred to by "names" which act as easily remembered references to variables stored in memory. Numeric variables are referred to by a single letter of the alphabet or a letter followed by a digit. Some versions of BASIC allow names to consist of a series of letters and digits, often unlimited in length. But, be careful,

1

sometimes only the first two letters are significant. All numeric variable names must start with a letter of the alphabet. In the examples in this book a convention is used with only one letter, or a letter followed by a digit as a variable name. Unless otherwise instructed numbers are stored in memory in four "bytes" - i.e. 4 x 8 = 32 binary digits. This enables numbers, positive or negative, in the range 10 nine digit accuracy to be stored. Some versions of BASIC allow "double precision" numbers to be stored. Double precision numbers are distinguished by a # sign after the variable name. They will, however, require twice as much memory space for each number since they are accurate to twice as many digits. As well as this some versions of BASIC allow numbers to be stored as integers - whole numbers - and these are distinguished by a % sign after their name. An integer only requires two bytes of memory for its storage.

A "string" of characters is allocated storage at the rate of one byte per character and a string variable is denoted by a dollar sign,$, after its name.

Examples:

Valid non-integer names: A,B1,D12,TOTAL,I,X0

Valid integer names: A%,I%,J8%,COUNT%

Valid double precision names: D#,VALUE#,MAX#

Valid string names: NAME$,ADDRESS$,F$,G1$

Symbols used in BASIC:

+	addition
-	subtraction
*	multiplication
/	division
^	exponentiation (raising to a power)
=	equal to
>	greater than
<	less than
>=	greater than or equal to

<=	less than or equal to
<>	not equal to
(	left hand bracket
)	right hand bracket
"	double quotes
,	comma
;	semi-colon
#	"hash" symbol (USA abbreviation for "number")

The brackets, quotation marks, comma and semi-colon are used as "delimiters".

NOTE: The = sign is used in two senses in BASIC. When used in a decision statement it is used to express the equality of two numbers. When used in an assignment statement it is used to stand for the words "takes the value of".

Assignment statements consist of a single variable name followed by = followed by an arithmetic expression:

e.g. Y = (4*X-3*D)/(2*H*L)

Only one variable name is allowed on the left of the = sign. The use of the keyword LET is optional before the first variable name - e.g.

LET Y = (4*X-3*D)/(2*H*L)

For integers we would write

H%=G1%-T4%

but beware of a statement such as

P%=Y%/R%

since the answer will only consist of the whole number part resulting from the division process. In other words, if Y% was 5 and R% was 2 then the value assigned to P% would be 2.

For string variables we could write

A$="GEORGE" - the actual characters to be

stored in the string variable A$ must be delimited by double quotation marks.

It is perfectly in order to write

S$=F$+V$

except that the resulting string stored in S$ would be the result of **concatenating** the string F$ with the string V$. This means that the second string is placed at the end of the first thus producing a longer string. For example if F$ was "HAPPY" and V$ was "DAYS" then S$ would contain the string "HAPPYDAYS".

The common BASIC keywords and examples of their uses are shown below:

KEYWORD	EXAMPLE	
LET	100	LET C = A + B - T
INPUT	200	INPUT X,Y,Z (INPUT receives data from the keyboard.)
	250	INPUT A$,NAME$
INPUT "text";	345	INPUT "NAME";N$
LINE INPUT	360	LINE INPUT A$ (This is used if the text being input contains commas.)
PRINT	300	PRINT C2,"IS THE ANSWER" (PRINT outputs to the video screen.)
READ	400	READ X,Y,D$ (READ takes data from a DATA line.)
DATA	500	DATA 23.45,89,"LONDON"
GOTO	600	GOTO 125 (The line numbered 125 must exist.)
IF..THEN..	700	IF(Assertion) THEN (BASIC statement)

Assertion is a statement of an equality or inequality such as

> X=Y
> C>=4
> A$="END"

but not

> X = "END"

or

> A$>5.6

The BASIC statement is any valid BASIC instruction such as

> GOTO 230

or

> PRINT "YES"

If the assertion is not true then the instruction following the THEN is not executed, and the instruction immediately following is executed instead. Some versions of BASIC allow the use of

> IF (Assertion) THEN (BASIC instruction) ELSE (BASIC instruction)

The first statement is executed if the assertion is true and the second if it is false. For example

> 250 IF X>A THEN PRINT "HIGH" ELSE PRINT "LOW"

AND   500 IF X=1 AND Y>0 THEN..........

(The AND conjunction is used as a logical operator to perform tests on multiple relations. It is used to make decisions connecting two or more relations and returns either **true** or **false** values of the assertion.)

OR   600 IF A$="YES" OR B$="YES" THEN..........

(Again the OR conjunction i used to perform a test on a multiple relationship.)

GOSUB   800 GOSUB 8000

RETURN   8000 RETURN
             (Returns to statement
              immediately following the
              GOSUB instruction.)

STOP   900 STOP
             (The program stops, but can
              usually be restarted by the
              command CONT.)

DIM	1000 DIM Y9(500),F$(50),B(3,10)

                        (Allocates 500 locations for the list Y9, 50 locations for the list of strings called F$ and sets up a table called B with 3 rows and 10 columns.)

END	1100 END

                        (Signifies the end of the program. Has a similar effect to STOP - usually optional.)

FOR..NEXT.	1200 FOR I%=1 TO 50 STEP 5
	1300 NEXT I%

                        (Looping instructions - execute the instructions within the FOR..NEXT loop in steps indicated by the STEP part of the instruction I% is the **control variable** in this case.)

REM	1400 REM --any text--

                        (REMarks do not affect the running of the program and are purely for information.)

DEF FNn	1500 DEF FNC(K)= K*3.5+56.8976

                        (A user-defined function referred to subsequently in a program by, say, 1800 X=FNC(J).)

More than one BASIC instruction can be written on a line; the colon (:) symbol is used to separate instructions written on a single line. For example:

100 FOR I = 1 TO 10:PRINT I:NEXT I

However, be careful not to attempt to make jumps to a statement which is in the middle of a line of multiple statements. Jumps can only be made to the first statement on a line.

BASIC allows a large number of functions which very often perform quite complicated tasks without any further action on the part of the programmer, such as:-

ABS(X)	Absolute value of X	
ATN(X)	Angle(in radians) whose tangent is X	
COS(X)	Cosine of angle X (in radians)	
EXP(X)	Exponential value of X (e^X)	
INT(X)	Largest integer less than or equal to X (Watch the effect of negative numbers)	
LOG(X)	Natural logarithm of X	
RND(X)	Random number in range 0 to 1 - sometimes the X is a dummy variable	
SGN(X)	1 if X is greater than zero 0 if X is zero -1 if X is less than zero	
SIN(X)	Sine of angle X (in radians)	
SPC(X)	Leave X spaces before printing next number	
SQR(X)	Square root of X	
TAB(X);Y	Tabs to position X before printing Y	
TAN(X)	Tangent of angle X (in radians)	
LEN(A$)	Number of characters in string A$	
LEFT$(A$,X)	The first X characters of string A$	
RIGHT$(A$,X)	The last X characters of string A$	
MID$(A$,X,Y)	The substring of the string A$ starting at the Xth character and Y characters long	
VAL(A$)	The numerical equivalent of the string A$	

If data is transferred between a file kept on disc, or magnetic tape, and memory there tends to be a wide selection of instructions available. The form of these instructions depends on the whim of the manufacturer and the reader is advised to refer to the manual supplied with the computer for the exact form of these instructions. However, these instructions will be of three types :

   (1) OPEN and CLOSE statements

   (2) INPUT and PRINT statements

   (3) Statements which allow the end of a sequential file to be detected

An OPEN statement will tell the program all about the file you are going to use. It usually consists of the name of the file, the logical number which is to be used whenever data is being transferred between the file and memory, and the **mode** of the file. The mode of the file is an instruction which tells the computer that the file is either to be written to or read from. A file which has been written to cannot be read from unless it has first been CLOSEd and then re-opened in the reading mode. All files must be CLOSEd at the end of a program.

In Microsoft(TM) BASIC a file is opened by the use of an OPEN statement which looks like this if the file is to be written to:

   OPEN "O",1,"FILENAME"

and like this if it is to be read from:

   OPEN "I",1,"FILENAME"

The letter in double quotes indicates the **mode** of the file; "O" for Output from memory to the file and "I" for Input from the file to memory. The number following the mode indication is called the **logical file number** and is the number used to reference the file subsequently in the program. The name by which the computer system refers to the file comes after the logical file number and is always enclosed in double quotes.

Data is transferred from a file into memory by means of an INPUT# instruction. This is of exactly the same format as the INPUT statement used to transfer data from keyboard to memory. The number after the # sign is the logical file number specified in the OPEN statement. In order to copy data from memory to a file we use the PRINT# instruction, where the number following the # is the logical file number of the file being PRINTed to. Now because this is a PRINT statement we have to separate the variables being printed by some sort of delimiter. For example we write:

500 PRINT A,B,C

when we want to print the values of the variables onto the video screen. When writing to a file we have to write

500 PRINT#1,A;",";B;",";C

The delimiters, the commas, have to be printed to the file as well as the data itself.

A sequential, or serial, file is read record by record and when the situation arises where the last record has been read the program will try to read beyond the end of the file and attempt to read whatever rubbish has been left there by some other program. In order to prevent this unwanted situation arising all BASIC systems will provide some form of end of file detector which usually takes the form of

200 IF EOF(2) THEN GOTO 500

which is saying "if you have read past the last intelligible record on the file go to line 500". If this test is not put in the program will stop and an error message will appear.

When reading from a serial file take care about the relative positions of the READ# and IF EOF instructions. In Microsoft(TM) BASIC the order of instructions is:

OPEN file for reading
IF EOF instruction
READ# instruction
Process the data read from the record
GOTO the IF EOF instruction
CLOSE instruction

Notice that the loop, in effect, has to remind the program what to do if the end of file is reached. This sequence is only, however, applicable to this particular version of BASIC. For other variations on this theme you could do well to consult "PROGRAM YOUR MICROCOMPUTER IN BASIC", P.E.Gosling, Macmillan 1981 - Activity 15.

Random access, or Direct access, files do not have to be read sequentially record by record from start to finish but allow the programmer to read to or write from any record directly. Hence reading and writing instructions which refer to direct access files must contain a parameter which defines the record being accessed at any time. An introduction to the use of random access files is given in the final chapter of this book.

Finally a word about some of the important BASIC commands. A **command** is a keyword which can always be used outside a program and sometimes within a program. Commands which are used outside a program are words such as:

       RUN   Execute the program currently in
                  memory.

       RUN nnnn   Run the current program starting at
                  line number nnnn.

       LIST   Copy the current program line by line
                  onto the video screen.

       LIST nnnn Copy the contents of line number nnnn
                  onto the video screen.

       LIST n1-n2 Copy the current program from line
                  number n1 to line number n2 onto
                  the video screen.

       LOAD   Copy a named program from backing
                  store into memory.

       SAVE   Save the program currently in memory
                  onto backing store under a specified
                  name.

       RENUM   Renumber the lines of the current
                  program in units of 10 starting at
                  the first line which is to be numbered
                  as line 10. All the GOTO, IF and GOSUB
                  statements are automatically adjusted.

The following statements can also be used within a program:

       KILL   Delete a named program from backing
                  store.

   NAME "PROG1" AS "PROG2"

                  Rename the program held on backing
                  store as "PROG1" to be now known
                  "PROG2".

Incorrect use of BASIC statements will always give rise to error messages of one sort or another and it is about these error messages and their causes that a large part of this book is about. Programming is easy when nothing goes wrong. When things go wrong we need to be able to trace the cause of the error and rectify it. The programs in the next section all produce error messages when you attempt to run them. Your job is to interpret the error messages you get and correct the mistakes which caused them. But watch out, the correction of one error can often uncover another. You have been warned.

2. Seeking out errors

Any manual which gives details of the version of the BASIC language applicable to a particular microcomputer will list the possible errors which can be detected and the messages which BASIC sends you on their detection. Some of these messages are fairly easy to understand; the word **syntax** covering a wide variety of errors in many cases but usually indicating that a misuse of the BASIC language has taken place. This often happens when keywords are either mis-spelt, used in the wrong way or keywords which do not exist in your version of the language have been used. The program listed in example 2.1 is a case in point.

```
10 IMPUT X
20 LET X*X=Y
30 OUTPUT Y
```

EXAMPLE 2.1

Here we have a program which contains both mis-spelling and an incorrect keyword. It also flouts the rules of BASIC in line 20; this is also detected as being a syntax error and the program will not progress beyond any line error until that error has been corrected. The program listed in example 2.2 is another example of mis-use of the BASIC language.

```
10 INPUT X
20 LET Y=4(X*X+3X-2)
30 PRINT Y
40 LET Y=X(X*X*X -2X*X+4)
50 PRINT Y
60 END
```

EXAMPLE 2.2

You should make sure that you appreciate why the error in line 40 is different from the error in line 20. The errors in example 2.3 are rather more subtle and require a certain amount of rewriting of the program before they can be eliminated.

```
10 INPUT A$:B$="                                    "
20 IF LEN(A$)<7 THEN 10
30 LEFT$(B$,4)=MID$(A$,3,4)
40 PRINT B$
```

EXAMPLE 2.3

The object of this program is to place a substring of the string A$ into a section of the string B$ which initially is filled with spaces. This problem will occur again in later examples in this section.

```
10 REM***THIS PROGRAM ACCEPTS NUMBERS AS INPUT BUT ONLY
   ADDS***
20 REM***THOSE BETWEEN 1 AND 10 INTO THE TOTAL***
30 INPUT X
40 IF X=0 THEN 70
50 IF 1<X<10 THEN S=S+X
60 GOTO 30
70 PRINT S
```

EXAMPLE 2.4

The program in example 2.4 is one where it all looks fine from a logical point of view but fails to work when run. The problem is in the IF statement which contains

IF 1<X<10 THEN....

which at first sight is quite easy to understand - but it is not. Look at the use of the AND conjunction and see if you can put the program right. Then you should try to find out just why the statement in the program is wrong.

```
5 PRINT "FIRST TIME"
6 PRINT
10 FOR X=-1 TO 1 STEP .1
20 LET Y=X*X+4*X-1/(X*X)
30 PRINT Y
40 NEXT X
41 PRINT
45 PRINT "SECOND PART"
50 FOR X= -1 TO 1 STEP .25
60 LET Y=X*X+4*X-1/(X*X)
70 PRINT Y
80 NEXT X
```

EXAMPLE 2.5

The error in example 2.5 is of the type known as a **run-time** error. This will only show up under certain conditions while the program is executing. It also highlights the need for a careful choice of test data when checking programs out.

```
10 REM***THIS PROGRAM CALCULATES MEAN AND STANDARD
   DEVIATION OF 20 NUMBERS***
20 FOR I=1 TO 20
30 READ X
40 T=T+X
50 NEXT I
60 PRINT T,T/20
70 FOR I=1 TO 20
80 READ X
90 S=S+X*X
100 NEXT I
110 PRINT S
120 A=S/20:B=T/20
130 C=A+B
140 S1=SQR(C*C)
150 PRINT S1
160 DATA 4,6,7,8,2,10,8,6,3,3,2,7,4,10,5,8,9,1
```

EXAMPLE 2.6

Example 2.6 is a case where a program has one error cloaking another. When the first, obvious, errors have been dealt with there is a need to check whether, in fact, the program is doing exactly what is required of it. This is another example of the need for test data which will produce a known output. Always check to see if the answer produced by a program which performs a mass of arithmetic is reasonable and acceptable.

Getting FOR...NEXT.... loops tied in a knot is a very common mistake to make and the program in example 2.7 is a case in point. The object is to print a table of four rows and three columns. As it stands the program will fail miserably, but the right ideas are there. All you need to do is to sort the loops out - or is it ?

```
1 REM***THIS PROGRAM READS AND PRINTS A TABLE WITH 4 RO!
  AND 3 COLUMNS*'
5 DIM A(4,3)
10 FOR I=1 TO 4
20 FOR J=1 TO 3
30 READ A(J,I)
40 NEXT I
50 NEXT J
60 FOR I=1 TO 3
70 FOR J=1 TO 3
80 PRINT A(J,I)
90 NEXT J
110 NEXT I
120 DATA 1,2,3,4,5,6,7,8,9,10,11,12
```

EXAMPLE 2.7

The program illustrated in example 2.8 is one which again looks fine, but may not work as you would expect it to, especially on small microcomputers.

```
10 FOR I=1 TO 200
20 S=S+.01
30 NEXT I
40 A(1)=1
50 A(2)=10
60 A(3)=100
70 PRINT A(S)
```

EXAMPLE 2.8

The errors thrown up by the programs in examples 2.9 and 2.10 are not so much mis-use of the language but more a case of not seeing wood for trees. The error in the first of these is a common one where the program writer gets the logic right but forgets that the computer is even more logical than he is.

```
5 REM***THIS PROGRAM DECIDES WHETHER A NUMBER IS ODD OR
  EVEN***
10 INPUT "TYPE IN A NUMBER";X
20 IF X/2=INT(X/2) THEN PRINT "THE NUMBER IS EVEN"
30 PRINT "THE NUMBER IS ODD"
```

EXAMPLE 2.9

```
10 INPUT A,B,C
20 FOR I=A TO B STEP C
30 PRINT I;
40 NEXT I
50 PRINT"EXIT VALUE: ";I
```

EXAMPLE 2.10

Example 2.10 is one where you can see just how your computer handles FOR...NEXT... loops. Run the program on more than one machine and you can see that you get widely differing answers. It all depends on the point in the program where the updating of the counting variables takes place. Try the program with some silly data to see how this is handled. You could be surprised at the result. See what happens if you make the control variable go from, say, 5 to 1 in steps of 1 - yes, 1 not -1 !

The rest of the programs in this section are all rather more complex than the previous ones and careful examination and in some cases trial and error testing is required to make them work as intended.

```
10 DIM K(20),X(15)
20 PRINT "type number of items"
30 INPUT N
40 PRINT"type items"
50 FOR J= 1 TO N
60 INPUT K(J),X(J)
70 NEXT J
80 PRINT"type in required key value"
90 INPUT A
100 IF A<X(1) THEN 240
110 IF A<X(N) THEN 240
120 L=0
130 H=N
140 K=H-L
150 IF K<2 THEN 240
160 M=H+L
170 M=INT(M/2)
180 IF A=K(M) THEN 260
190 IF A<K(M) THEN 220
200 L=M
210 GOTO 140
220 H=M
230 GOTO 160
240 PRINT"ITEM NOT FOUND
250 GOTO 270
260 PRINT"ITEM FOUND";" ";K(M);" ";X(M)
270 PRINT "ANOTHER SEARCH , YES OR NO"
280 INPUT A$
290 IF A$="YES" THEN 80
300 END
```

EXAMPLE 2.11

Example 2.11 is a program which has been designed to read up to 20 "records", each consisting of a unique numerical key followed by a number. The program should then accept a series of requests to locate and print the number corresponding to a specified key. The listing of the program contains errors on exactly four lines. You should be able to identify these errors and correct them. In addition the program is unsatisfactory in that although it requires the input list to be in numerical order of keys it does not check to see if this is so. You should write an additional section of program which will check that the input list is in fact in order. Remember that you should try and make the program as "friendly" to the user as possible so that it should be made clear that the input list is not in the required order and should be checked before proceeding further.

The next program, shown in example 2.12, is one which arranges for a maximum of 500 accounts to be stored in a list called T.

```
20 DIM T(500)
30 FOR I=1 TO 500
40 T(I)=0
50 NEXT I
60 Y=0
70 PRINT "TYPE OF OPERATION AND ACCOUNT CODE"
80 INPUT F$,A
90 I=1+A-500*INT(A)/500
100 I=P
110 IF F$="INSERT" THEN 180
120 IF F$="SEARCH" THEN 290
130 IF F$="DELETE" THEN 290
140 IF F$="STOP" THEN 290
150 PRINT "INVALID OPERATION"
160 GOTO 70
170 REM***INSERTION***
180 IF T(I)>0 THEN 220
190 T(I)=A
200 PRINT "ITEM PUT IN LOCATION :";I
210 GOTO 70
220 LET I=I+1
230 IF I<250 THEN 250
240 LET I=I+1
250 IF I<>P THEN 180
260 PRINT "TABLE FULL"
270 GOTO 70
280 REM***FIND ENTRY***
290 GOSUB 380
300 IF Y=1 THEN 70
310 IF F$="DELETE" THEN 340
320 PRINT "ITEM FOUND IN LOCATION :";I
330 GOTO 70
340 REM***DELETION***
350 LET T(I)=-1
360 PRINT "ITEM FOUND AND DELETED FROM LOCATION :";I
370 GOTO 70
380 REM***SUBROUTINE SEARCH***
390 IF T(I)<>A THEN 460
400 LET I=I-1
410 IF I>=500 THEN 430
420 LET I=1
430 IF I<>P THEN 390
440 PRINT "ITEM NOT FOUND"
450 Y=1
460 RETURN
470 END
```

EXAMPLE 2.12

The position of an account in the list is determined by the account code using a method called **hash** coding. The position of an account in the list is calculated by dividing the number, called A, by 500 and taking the integer part of the answer. This number is then multiplied by 500 and subtracted from 1+A. This is called the hashing **rule** and gives the location of the record in the list. In other words, if A is 1452 then the record is placed in the record numbered

$$1+A-500*2 = 453$$

since 1452 divided by 500 gives 2.904 giving a whole number part of 2. However, it is likely that two entries might finish up with the same hash value. In this case the next location is tried. If that is empty then the data is placed in that record. If it is already occupied then the next in sequence is tried, and so on. Eventually either the entire table is found to be full or a vacant "slot" is found for the data. By using a hashing rule such as this it is possible to locate an entry in a table without having to search the table from the first entry every time. Hashing saves a lot of searching time since the hashing rule is used to give the position of the first record to be examined in order to find the required data. The program illustrated contains a number of errors. There are eight in the listing given and in addition there is one line which is in the wrong place. When the program has been amended it should work as shown in example 2.12a.

```
>TYPE OF OPERATION AND ACCOUNT CODE
INSERT, 1452
ITEM PUT IN LOCATION : 453
TYPE OF OPERATION AND ACCOUNT CODE
INSERT, 1453
ITEM PUT IN LOCATION : 454
TYPE OF OPERATION AND ACCOUNT CODE
INSERT, 1501
ITEM PUT IN LOCATION : 2
TYPE OF OPERATION AND ACCOUNT CODE
INSERT, 1504
ITEM PUT IN LOCATION : 5
TYPE OF OPERATION AND ACCOUNT CODE
INSERT, 2314
ITEM PUT IN LOCATION : 315
TYPE OF OPERATION AND ACCOUNT CODE
SEARCH, 1452
ITEM FOUND IN LOCATION : 453
TYPE OF OPERATION AND ACCOUNT CODE
DELETE, 1452
ITEM FOUND AND DELETED FROM LOCATION : 453
TYPE OF OPERATION AND ACCOUNT CODE
SEARCH, 1452
ITEM NOT FOUND
TYPE OF OPERATION AND ACCOUNT CODE
INSERT, 1452
ITEM PUT IN LOCATION : 453
TYPE OF OPERATION AND ACCOUNT CODE
STOP, 0
```

EXAMPLE 2.12a

Now for a program which deals with strings. In order to economise on memory it is sometimes useful to pack a list of names, or other sets of characters, into a single string and provide access to these names by means of **access vectors**. These act as pointers to the position of the names inside the string and consist of a series of numbers held in a list, called F in our example, which points to the first character of each name within the strings and another list called L which holds the length of each name. For example, if a string A$ contains the characters

"GEORGETOMSARAFREDJANE"

then the list F would contain the following numbers

```
F(1) = 1
F(2) = 7
F(3) = 10
F(4) = 14
F(5) = 18
```

and the list L would be arranged as

```
L(1) = 6
L(2) = 3
L(3) = 4
L(4) = 4
L(5) = 4
```

It then becomes a simple task to sort the access vectors in order to make them point to the names in their alphabetical order leaving the actual names in the string A$ unmoved. After the sorting process the new form of the lists would be

```
F(1) = 14
F(2) = 1
F(3) = 18
F(4) = 10
F(5) = 7
```

and

```
L(1) = 4
L(2) = 6
L(3) = 4
L(4) = 4
L(5) = 3
```

```
100 DIM F(30)
105 I=1:J=1
120 INPUT X
130 REM***TEST FOR END OF THE LIST***
```

```
140 IF X="ZZZ" THEN 310
150 A$=A$+X$
160 F(J)=I
170 L(J)=LEN(A$)
180 I=I+LEN(X$)
190 J=J+1
200 PRINT "LAST NAME REJECTED - OVERFLOW OF A$ - DO YOU
    WISH TO PROCEED"
201 REM***MAX LENGTH OF THE STRING DEPENDS ON THE SYSTEM
    YOU USE***
210 PRINT "TO SORT, YES OR NO ";
220 INPUT X$
230 ***REM GOTO THE END UNLESS "YES" HAS BEEN CORRECTLY
    INPUT***
240 IF X$="YES" THEN 480
250 REM
260 REM***SORT THE LIST OF NAMES***
310 FOR I=1 TO J-2
320 K=I
330 IF K>=0 THEN 430
340 REM***COMPARE NAMES ADJACENT IN ACCESS VECTOR***
350 IF MID$(A$,F(K),L(K))<= MID$(A$,F(K+1),L(K+1))
    THEN 430
360 REM***SWAP VECTOR VALUES IF NECESSARY***
370 C=F(K)
380 F(K)=F(K+1)
390 F(K+1)=C
400 C=L(K)
430 NEXT I
440 PRINT
450 FOR I=1 TO J-1
460 PRINT MID$(A$,F(I),L(I))
470 NEXT I
480 END
```

EXAMPLE 2.13

A program which attempts to do this is shown in example 2.13. However there are a number of errors which prevent the program from working properly. These consist of several lines which have been omitted and four of the lines of the program containing errors. When the program has been amended the output should look as shown in example 2.13a.

```
? JOHN
? NIGEL
? JANE
? SIMON
? MICHAEL
? SARAH
? ANN
? TONY
? XENIA
? BOB
```

```
? ZZZ
ANN
BOB
JANE
JOHN
MICHAEL
NIGEL
SARAH
SIMON
TONY
XENIA
```

EXAMPLE 2.13a

```
30 P$=".!,;"
40 READ A$
50 L=LEN(A$)
60 N=1
70 FOR I=1 TO L
80 IF MID$(A$,I,1)<>" " THEN 140
90 IF S=0 THEN 250
100 MID$(B$,N,1)=" "
110 N=N+1
120 S=0
130 GOTO 250
140 FOR J=1 TO 4
150 IF MID$(A$,I,1)<>MID$(P$,J,1)THEN 210
160 MID$(B$,N,1)=MID$(P$,J,1)
170 MID$(B$,N1,1)=" "
180 N=N1
190 S=0
200 GOTO 250
210 NEXT J
220 MID$(B$,N1,1)=MID$(A$,I,1)
230 N=N1
240 S=1
250 NEXT I
260 PRINT B$
270 END
280 DATA"  GOOD   SHOT,SIR !"
290 DATA"GOAL   !!"
300 DATA"  OH! THAT'S   SUPER,THANKS  ?"
```

EXAMPLE 2.14

Example 2.14 is a program which attempts to edit a piece of text according to the following rules:

(1) Spaces before the start of the text are deleted.

(2) Any multiple spaces are reduced to a single space.

(3) A punctuation mark such as ,;.or ! is to be followed by a single space unless it ends the text.

For example, if the text was

" GOOD   SHOT,SIR !"

it should become

"GOOD SHOT, SIR !"

It is assumed that the data is always correctly input into the program and the text always ends with a punctuation mark. The program as listed in example 2.14 contains a number of errors and omissions. If you amend the program correctly you should get output as shown in example 2.14a.

```
 GOOD   SHOT,SIR !
GOOD SHOT, SIR !
GOAL   !!
GOAL ! !
 OH! THAT'S   SUPER,THANKS  ?
OH! THAT'S SUPER, THANKS ?
```

EXAMPLE 2.14a

```
10 REM***WHEN USING THIS REMEMBER THAT A SPACE IS A
   CHARACTER***
110 C1=1
120 PRINT "TYPE IN THE STRING TO BE EDITED"
125 INPUT C$
130 PRINT "COMMAND"
140 INPUT I
150 I=0
160 IF I$="EXCHANGE" THEN 290
170 I=I+1
180 IF I$="INSERT AFTER" THEN 290
190 I=I+1
200 IF I$="INSERT BEFORE" THEN 290
210 IF I$="STOP" THEN 660
220 PRINT"INVALID INSTRUCTION";
230 IF C1=4 THEN 270
240 C1=C1+1
250 PRINT "TRY AGAIN"
260 GOTO 130
270 PRINT "TOO MANY TRIES"
280 STOP
290 C1=1
300 PRINT "INPUT FIRST STRING"
310 INPUT A$
320 PRINT "INPUT SECOND STRING"
```

```
330 INPUT B$
340 C=LEN(C$)
350 A=LEN(A$)
360 B=LEN(B$
370 IF I=0 THEN 410
380 IF C-B+A>255 THEN 640
390 GOTO 410
400 IF C+B>255 THEN 640
410 J=J+1
420 IF MID$(C$,J,1)<>LEFT$(A$,1) THEN 440
430 IF MID$(C$,J,A)<>A$ THEN 470
440 IF J=C-A+1 THEN 620
450 J=J+1
460 GOTO 410
470 J=J
480 IF J=1 THEN 500
490 O$=LEFT$(C$,J-1)
500 IF I<>1 THEN 580
510 O$=O$+A$
520 J=J+A
530 O$=O$+B$
540 J=J+B
550 IF I<>2 THEN 580
560 O$=O$+A$
570 J=J+A
580 O$=O$+RIGHT$(C$,LEN(C$)-P-A+1)
590 PRINT O$
600 C$=O$
610 GOTO 130
620 PRINT A$ NOT FOUND IN C$
630 GOTO 130
660 END
```

EXAMPLE 2.15

Another text editing program is shown in example 2.15. The object of this program is to edit a piece of text in the following ways:

(1) EXCHANGE one set of characters in the text for another. The two sets of characters need not be of the same length.

(2) INSERT a new string AFTER a specified string in the text.

(3) INSERT a new string BEFORE a specified string in the text.

The commands to be interpreted by the program are therefore

EXCHANGE, INSERT AFTER, INSERT BEFORE and STOP.

The last command, of course, stops the program. Note that the exchange or insertion is made at the first occurrence of the specified string only. The program shown in the example contains ten lines which contain errors, some of which are obvious, others not so obvious. The print-out shown in example 2.15a shows a

```
TYPE IN THE STRING TO BE EDITED
NOW IS THE HOUR
COMMAND
EXCHANGE
INPUT FIRST STRING
THE
INPUT SECOND STRING
ANOTHER
NOW IS ANOTHER HOUR
COMMAND
INSERT BEFORE
INPUT FIRST STRING
HOUR
INPUT SECOND STRING
BRIGHT
NOW IS ANOTHER BRIGHTHOUR
COMMAND
INSERT AFTER
INPUT FIRST STRING
BRIGHT
INPUT SECOND STRING
 HAPPY
NOW IS ANOTHER BRIGHT HAPPYHOUR
COMMAND
STOP
```

EXAMPLE 2.15a

corrected version of the program at work. You should be able to improve the program even further by making it possible to change every occurrence of a particular string for another string - i.e. change every occurence of "TORY" to" LABOUR" or every "L" into "LL". The second of these can cause a few unexpected problems if not handled carefully.

The editing of text forms a very important part of computing these days and the example shown next gives some idea of the problems involved in writing programs to achieve this.

```
15 P$=""
20 PRINT "INPUT SENTENCE"
30 INPUT X$
40 PRINT "INPUT WORD TO BE REPLACED"
50 INPUT A$
60 PRINT "INPUT NEW WORD"
70 INPUT B$
80 X=LEN(X$)
90 A=LEN(A$)
```

```
100 B=LEN(B$)
110 S=A-B
120 J=1
130 I=1
140 M=1
150 IF MID$(X$,J,1)<>LEFT$(A$,1) THEN 170
160 IF MID$(X$,J,A)= A$ THEN 240
170 J=J+1
180 IF J<=X THEN 150
190 IF I>1 THEN 220
200 PRINT A$;" NOT FOUND IN ";X$
210 STOP
220 PRINT P$;RIGHT$(X$,X-M+1)
230 STOP
280 IF S>=0 THEN 320
290 IF I+J-M+B-1 <255 THEN 320
300 PRINT "INTERSECTION OF B$ MAKES LENGTH OF P$>255
    CHARACTERS"
310 STOP
320 IF J=1 THEN 350
380 M=J
390 GOTO 170
400 END
```

EXAMPLE 2.16

Example 2.16 shows a program whose object is to replace one set of characters in a string by another set of characters. For example the string

"THE PERFORMER WENT TO THE THEATRE"

could be amended by this program by the replacement of every occurrence of the word "THE" by "A". But be careful, because the example has been chosen carefully. The string "THE" is not only a separate word in the text but is also a part of the word "THEATRE". It is only the separate "THE" which has to be changed, not every set of the characters "THE". This can be done in several ways, but in this program it is done according to the flowchart shown in example 2.16a. The output you should get from an amended version of the program is shown in example 2.16b. The listed program has a number of important lines missing and these lie between lines 230 to 280 and lines 320 to 380.

The next problem involves a rather more detailed look at the technique used in example 2.12. Here the hash coding is actually applied to the storage and retrieval of records which refer to students of the Open University. The details of the students are recorded in lists of strings called A$,B$,C$ and D$. A$ is a list of names, B$ is a list of towns, C$ is a list of counties and D$ is a list of the student reference numbers. For the sake of simplicity only thirty records

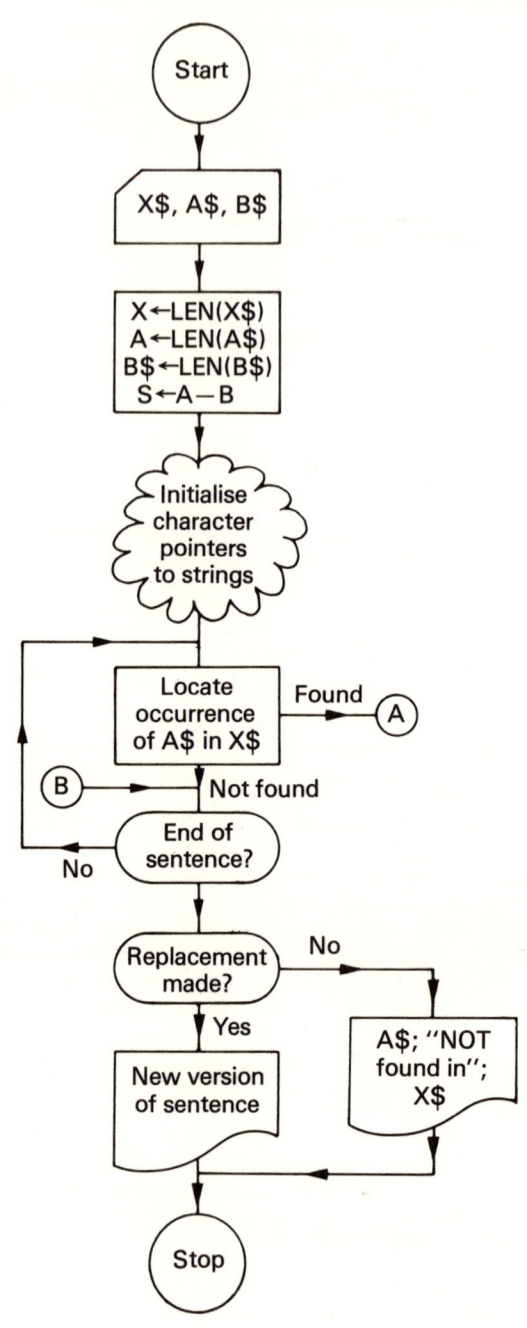

EXAMPLE 2.16a

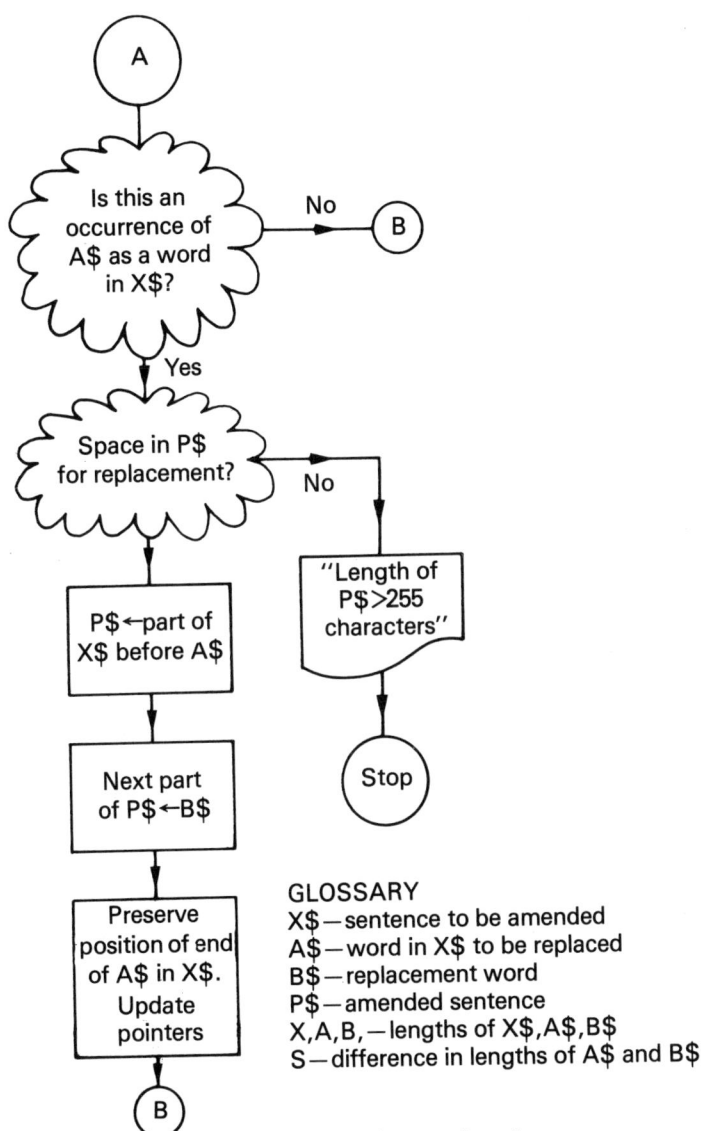

EXAMPLE 2.16a continued

```
INPUT SENTENCE
?THE PERFORMER WENT TO THE THEATRE
INPUT WORD TO BE REPLACED
?THE
INPUT NEW WORD
?A
A PERFORMER WENT TO A THEATRE
```

EXAMPLE 2.16b

are stored in the lists and the first ten of these are illustrated in the diagram shown in example 2.17. In order to find the record corresponding to a given student number a vector, H which contains a list of 30 numbers, provides an index. Each element of H can contain a number of a record in each list. For example H(9) contains the number 7, as shown in the diagram, and the seventh item in each list contains the information relating to student number Y892447.

The vector H is set up by applying the following procedure to each record in the lists in turn:

(1) Apply a given hashing rule to the student number in order to produce a hash value in the range 1 to 30 inclusive.
(2) Store the record number in vector H in the location corresponding to its hash value.

The hashing rule used is as follows:

(a) Allocate a number to each character in the student number string. The characters 0-9 are converted into the corresponding numbers 0-9 while the numbers 10-35 are allotted to the characters A-Z respectively.
(b) Convert the sum of all these numbers to an integer in the range 10 to 30 inclusive by dividing this sum by 30 and adding one to the remainder. For example, 57 divided by 30 gives remainder 27. Adding one to this gives a hash value of 28.

As an example of this procedure, the 7th element of A$ contains the name of student number Y892447. The 7th element of B$ contains his town. The 7th element of C$ contains his county and the 7th element of D$ contains his student number. Note that if H(9) had already been used then 7 would have been placed in the first available unused location after H(9). For this purpose H(1) would be considered to be the location immediately following location H(30). The flowchart shown in example 2.17a shows how the vector H is set up.

The program which is intended to set up the vector H and also search for student numbers is shown in example 2.17b.

```
100 DIM H(30),A$(30),B$(30),C$(30),D(30)
150 FOR I=1 TO 10
160 READ A$(I),B$(I),C$(I),D$(I)
210 F=0
220 I$=D$(I)
```

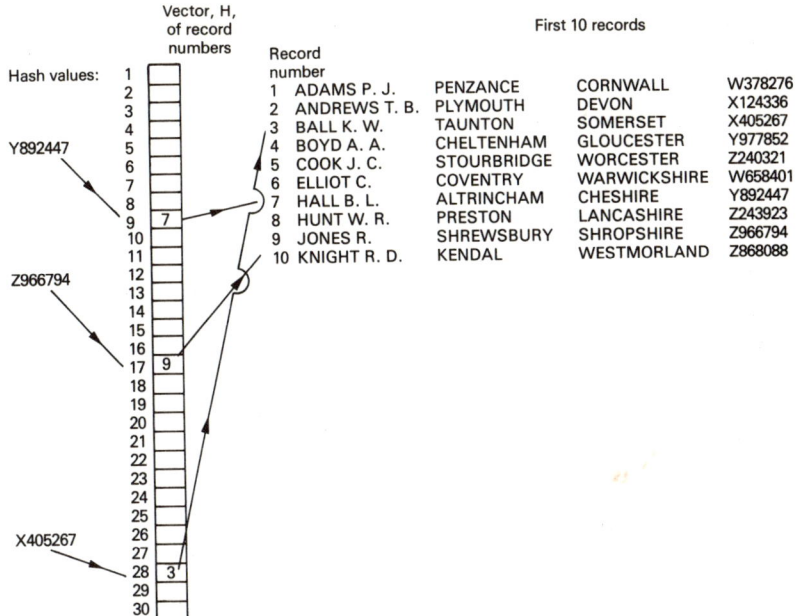

Figure 2.17

```
230 GOSUB 680
240 IF F=1 THEN 350
250 R=V
260 A=R
270 IF H(A)=0 THEN 340
280 A=A+1-INT(A/30)*30
290 IF A<>R THEN 270
300 PRINT "HASH TABLE FULL"
310 REM *** THIS CANNOT HAPPEN IN THIS EXAMPLE BUT THE
    CASE IS ***
320 REM *** INCLUDED FOR COMPLETENESS
330 GOTO 350
340 H(A)=I
350 NEXT I
360 PRINT "INDEX     RECORD NUMBER     STUDENT NUMBER"
370 FOR I = 1 TO 30
380 IF H(I)= 0 THEN 410
390 PRINT I,H(I),D$(H(I))
410 NEXT I
420 PRINT
430 PRINT
440 PRINT "DO YOU WISH TO SEARCH THE TABLE FOR STUDENT
    NUMBERS, YES OR NO "
450 INPUT X$
460 IF X$="NO" THEN 660
470 PRINT
480 PRINT "INPUT STUDENT NUMBER"
490 INPUT X$
```

```
500 IF X$= "ZZZZ" THEN 660
640 PRINT A$(H(A));TAB(19);B$(H(A));TAB(39);C$(H(A))
650 GOTO 470
660 STOP
670 REM ***SUBROUTINE TO GENERATE HASH VALUES ***
680 M$="0123456789ABCDEFGHIJKLMNOPQRSTUVWXYZ"
690 V=0
700 FOR J= 1 TO 7
```

Glossary
H — vector holding record numbers
A$ — name string
B$ — town string
C$ — county string
D$ — student no. string
R — hash value
A — address currently in use in H
F — error flag for invalid student numbers

Figure 2.17a

```
710 T$=MID$(I$,J,1)
720 P=1
730 Q=36
740 IF Q<P THEN 870
750 R1=INT((P+Q)/2)
760 IF T$=MID$(M$,R1,1) THEN 820
770 IF T$<MID$(M$,R1,1) THEN 800
780 P=R1+1
790 GOTO 740
800 Q=R1-1
810 GOTO 740
820 V=V+R1-1
```

```
830 NEXT J
840 REM ***CONVERT HASH VALUE TO RANGE 1 TO 30***
850 V=V+1-INT(V/30)*30
860 RETURN
870 PRINT "INVALID STUDENT NUMBER"
880 F=1
890 RETURN
900 END
1000 DATA ADAMS.P.J.,PENZANCE,CORNWALL,W378276
1001 DATA ANDREWS.T.B.,PLYMOUTH,DEVON,X124336
1002 DATA BALL.K.W.,TAUNTON,SOMERSET,X405267
1003 DATA BOYD.A.A.,CHELTENHAM,GLOUCESTERSHIRE,Y977852
1004 DATA COOK.J.C.,STOURBRIDGE,WORCESTERSHIRE,Z240321
1005 DATA ELLIOT.C.,COVENTRY,WARWICKSHIRE,W658401
1006 DATA HALL.B.L.,ALTRINGHAM,CHESHIRE,Y892447
1007 DATA HUNT.W.R.,PRESTON,LANCASHIRE,Z243923
1008 DATA JONES.R.,SHREWSBURY,SHROPSHIRE,Z966794
1009 DATA KNIGHT.R.D.,KENDAL,WESTMORELAND,Z868088
```

EXAMPLE 2.17b

This program is incomplete and has had instructions omitted between lines 110 and 150 and lines 500 and 640. The proper operation of the program is shown in example 2.17c and your amended program should produce exactly the same results for the input used in that example.

INDEX	RECORD NUMBER	STUDENT NUMBER
6	1	W378276
9	7	Y892447
13	4	Y977852
14	10	Z868088
17	9	Z966794
18	5	Z240321
23	2	X124336
27	6	W658401
28	3	X405267
29	8	Z243923

```
DO YOU WISH TO SEARCH THE TABLE FOR STUDENT NUMBERS, YES
OR NO ? YES

INPUT STUDENT NUMBER?X450267
STUDENT RECORD NOT FOUND FOR THIS NUMBER

INPUT STUDENT NUMBER?Z996794
STUDENT RECORD NOT FOUND FOR THIS NUMBER

INPUT STUDENT NUMBER?Z966794
JONES.R.              SHREWSBURY              SHROPSHIRE

INPUT STUDENT NUMBER?ZZZZ
```

EXAMPLE 2.17c

3. Some simple programming problems

This section suggests a number of real life problems for you to try. Each one of them is presented as a statement of a problem, some suggestions of the approach you could make towards the solution, the test data you could try with your finished program and a speciment of the results you should get when the suggested data is used with your program.

Problem 3.1

A salesman is paid commission on the sales he makes according to the following rule:

SALES	COMMISSION
Up to £50 000	1.5% of the value of the sales
Between £50 000 and £100 000	1.5% of the first £50 000 plus 1% of the sales in that band
Between £100 000 and £150 000	1.5% of the first £50 000 plus 1% of the next £50 000 plus 0.5% of the sales in that band
Over £150 000	1.5% of the first £50 000 plus 1% of the next £50 000 plus 0.5% of the next £50 000 plus 0.25% of all sales over £150 000

In addition to his commission he is allowed £35.00 per week for motoring expenses and £40.00 per week for other expenses. His total expenses are allowed to rise by 10% per year for every year he is employed, based on his first year's expenses. Mr J.M.Smith was first employed in 1975 and in that year made sales of £80 000. In the following years his sales were £120 000, £160 000, £205 000 and £325 000. Your program should print out his income from expenses and commission for the years 1975, 1976, 1977, 1978 and 1979.

Before you start writing the program you must make sure that you understand exactly what is expected of it. You must be prepared to sit and think about the problem for some time and then sketch out a plan of action. Draw an outline flowchart of the type shown in figure 3.1 which gives an idea of the kind of procedures required. Notice that you have to be very precise about what "up to £50 000" really means. In

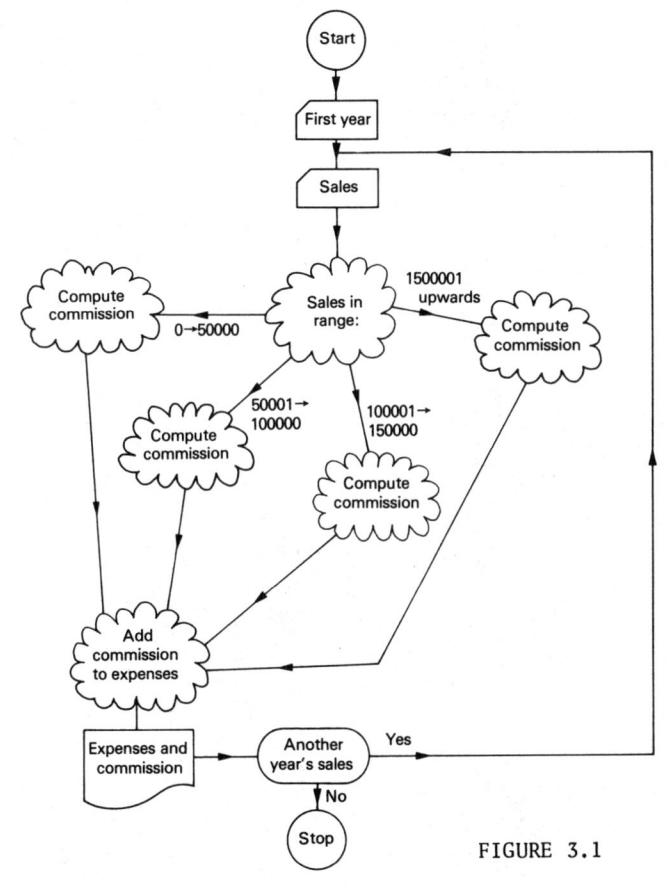

FIGURE 3.1

this case it should be taken as meaning "up to and including £50 000", which is not the same as "up to £50 000". The same applies to the rest of the bands of commission earned. You must always read every question carefully and make sure you have got the right interpretation of the problem it poses.

Having drawn an outline then a detailed flowchart should be produced and from this the final program can be written. It is not recommended that you just sit down at a keyboard and write the program without making fairly detailed notes first.

```
1000 DATA 1975,80000
1001 DATA 120000,160000,205000,325000,0
```

FIGURE 3.1a

The only data you need is shown in figure 3.1a and the output from the program should be as in figure 3.1b. Note the setting out and the headings of

```
J.M.SMITH - SUMMARY OF EARNINGS
--------------------------------
YEAR 1975
TOTAL EARNINGS £  4,950.00
COMMISSION     £  1,050.00
EXPENSES       £  3,900.00


YEAR 1976
TOTAL EARNINGS £  4,789.00
COMMISSION     £    850.00
EXPENSES       £  3,939.00


YEAR 1977
TOTAL EARNINGS £  5,503.39
COMMISSION     £  1,525.00
EXPENSES       £  3,978.39


YEAR 1978
TOTAL EARNINGS £  5,655.67
COMMISSION     £  1,637.50
EXPENSES       £  4,018.17


YEAR 1979
TOTAL EARNINGS £  5,995.86
COMMISSION     £  1,937.50
EXPENSES       £  4,058.36
```

FIGURE 3.1b

the output. Making the results from a program easy to understand is as important a part of the programming as the logic of the program itself.

Problem 3.2

A small firm employs 10 people and the pay of each of these is calculated according to a simple rule each week. The rule is that all time up to and including 40 hours is paid at a rate appropriate to each man. This rate is in pence per hour. If any work is done which takes the employee over 40 hours then this is paid at time and a half. The test data is shown in figure 3.2. Notice that it consists of the

```
2000 DATA 40,10
2001 DATA 1234,41,169.5
2002 DATA 2245,50,175
2003 DATA 2341,23,167.5
2004 DATA 3215,40.5,175
2005 DATA 3546,60,180
2006 DATA 4354,27.5,189.4
2007 DATA 4673,49.5,170
2008 DATA 6674,39.5,166.5
2009 DATA 7659,55.5,177.5
2010 DATA 5564,40,175.5
```

FIGURE 3.2

employee's clock number, the number of hours worked in one week and his rate of pay in pence. The first two pieces of data are the week number and the number of employees who worked that week. Note that the data consists of working hours of 40, just under 40, just over 40 and zero. The test data should cover all the possibilities to be covered by the program. The output is shown in figure 3.2a. Note that in this case we are dealing with money and we need to ensure that the pounds and pence are properly lined up. We also want to avoid amounts of money such as £45.8976 which should be properly rounded to £45.90. This is not always easy to do, but if your version of BASIC has the PRINT USING statement then this is a good time to get to know how it is used.

```
S.W.R.SUMMERS (ENGINEERING) LTD         WEEK NO: 40

CLOCK NUMBER     HOURS      RATE IN PENCE        PAY

   1234          41.0          169.5            70.34
   2245          50.0          175              96.25
   2341          23.0          167.5            38.53
   3215          40.5          175              71.31
   3546          60.0          180             126.00
   4354          27.5          189.4            52.09
   4673          49.5          170              92.23
   6674          39.5          166.5            65.77
   7659          55.5          177.5           112.27
   5564          40.0          175.5            70.20

HIGHEST WAGE :-
   3546          60            180             126.00

LOWEST WAGE :-
   2341          23            167.5            38.53
```

FIGURE 3.2a

A word of advice about the detailed writing of this program. It really consists of three parts. The first and most important is the actual construction of the payroll table itself. Make sure that you get this part finished and working before you go on to the rest of the problem. When you have satisfactorily solved the problem of the setting out of the payroll then you can look to the problems of discovering the highest and the lowest paypackets of the week. You can in fact separate this from the main problem by saying to yourself "how can I discover the largest, or smallest, number in a list ?" This can be done, in fact, by means of the simple program shown in figure 3.2b. It works because of the fact that computers cannot deal with anything more than one number at a time. So that when the first number in a list is presented to a computer it has no idea of what is coming and hence that number, at that time, must be the largest, and indeed the smallest, number in the list. All the numbers which follow can then be tested against the current largest or smallest. After the list has been examined from start to finish the largest, or smallest, can be printed out.

```
10 DIM A(100)
20 FOR I=1 TO 100
30 READ X
40 IF X=0 THEN 70
50 A(I)=X
60 NEXT I
70 L=A(1):S=A(1)
80 REM***THIS LINE COULD GIVE THE WRONG ANSWER IF YOU USE***
90 REM***SOME VERSIONS OF BASIC - SEE EXAMPLE 2.7***
100 N=I-1
110 PRINT
120 FOR I=2 TO N
130 IF A(I)>L THEN L=A(I)
140 IF A(I)<S THEN S=A(I)
150 NEXT I
160 PRINT"THE LARGEST IS :";L;"AND THE SMALLEST IS :";S
170 DATA 56,32,12,11,67,78,89,65,54,33,22,45,68,98,2,10,15,4
180 DATA 0
```

FIGURE 3.2b

Problem 3.3

This is another problem about a payroll, but it is rather more complex than the previous problem. The workers, who are named this time, work a 35-hour week. If they work at weekends they get paid double time and if they work overtime during the week they are paid time and a half. If they are off sick then they are paid sick pay of £8.00 per day. If, however, they have not worked 35 hours during the week but do work at weekends then they only get their normal rate of pay

for those hours. Note all the possible alternatives so
you will have to be very careful when you set up your
decisions. The output this time is in the form of a
statement for each man. Figure 3.3 shows the data you
should use and figure 3.3a shows the output you should
get with that data.

```
200 DATA FORBES,1224,36,0,0,1.60
210 DATA JONES,2346,10,3,0,1.85
220 DATA BROWN,5678,40,0,6,2.10
230 DATA JACKSON,9678,20,1,5,1.65
240 DATA YOUNG,3421,45,0,8,1.70
250 DATA WONG,6969,40,0,12,2.00
260 DATA SINGH,1919,36,0,10,2.10
270 DATA O'DAY,5670,28,1,4,2.00
280 DATA HARRISON,6491,50,0,6,1.65
290 DATA GRACE, 3345,21,1,10,1.98
```

FIGURE 3.3

PAYSLIPS FOR EMPLOYEES AT T.H.HOBSON LTD.

NAME: FORBES

CLOCK NUMBER:1224

HOURS WORKED : 36

DAYS OFF SICK: 0

RATE OF PAY:£1.60 PER HOUR

W/END HOURS WORKED: 0

TOTAL PAY £ 58.40

NAME: JONES

CLOCK NUMBER:2346

HOURS WORKED : 10

DAYS OFF SICK: 3

RATE OF PAY:£1.85 PER HOUR

W/END HOURS WORKED: 0

TOTAL PAY £ 42.50

NAME: BROWN

CLOCK NUMBER:5678

HOURS WORKED : 40

DAYS OFF SICK: 0

RATE OF PAY:£2.10 PER HOUR

W/END HOURS WORKED: 6

TOTAL PAY £114.45

NAME: JACKSON

CLOCK NUMBER:9678

HOURS WORKED : 20

DAYS OFF SICK: 1

RATE OF PAY:£1.65 PER HOUR

W/END HOURS WORKED: 5

TOTAL PAY £ 49.25

NAME: YOUNG

CLOCK NUMBER:3421

HOURS WORKED : 45

DAYS OFF SICK: 0

RATE OF PAY:£1.70 PER HOUR

W/END HOURS WORKED: 8

TOTAL PAY £112.20

NAME: WONG

CLOCK NUMBER:6969

HOURS WORKED : 40

DAYS OFF SICK: 0

RATE OF PAY:£2.00 PER HOUR

W/END HOURS WORKED: 12

TOTAL PAY £133.00

NAME: SINGH

CLOCK NUMBER:1919

HOURS WORKED : 36

DAYS OFF SICK: 0

RATE OF PAY:£2.10 PER HOUR

W/END HOURS WORKED: 10

TOTAL PAY £118.65

NAME: O'DAY

CLOCK NUMBER:5670

HOURS WORKED : 28

DAYS OFF SICK: 1

RATE OF PAY:£2.00 PER HOUR

W/END HOURS WORKED: 4

TOTAL PAY £ 72.00

NAME: HARRISON

CLOCK NUMBER:6491

HOURS WORKED : 50

DAYS OFF SICK: 0

RATE OF PAY:£1.65 PER HOUR

W/END HOURS WORKED: 6

TOTAL PAY £114.68

```
NAME: GRACE

CLOCK NUMBER:3345

HOURS WORKED : 21

DAYS OFF SICK: 1

RATE OF PAY:£1.98 PER HOUR

W/END HOURS WORKED: 10

TOTAL PAY £ 69.38
```

FIGURE 3.3a

Problem 3.4

Another problem about salesmen which will require you to use arrays of numbers. The program is to analyse the sales of a number of car salesmen who work for a chain of garages. The data consists of the number of cars sold by each man each month for a year. The output needs to record the yearly sales of each man and his average monthly sales. The program should be able to handle the data from up to 50 salesmen and the maximum number of cars sold per month by each man is 99. The data consists of the name of each man and the sales each month from January to December. This data is prefixed by the number of salesmen employed and is shown in figure 3.4. The output from the program

```
1000 DATA 6
1010 DATA 13,23,14,11,16,17,18,12,13,19,10,21
1020 DATA 3,6,8,19,21,20,12,13,15,16,17,18
1030 DATA 12,10,13,13,15,17,18,1,13,14,16,18
1040 DATA 5,6,7,8,3,2,5,4,0,2,1,7
1050 DATA 10,19,16,15,14,16,18,18,19,20,17,10
1060 DATA 6,7,12,13,15,16,17,18,23,24,25,21
```

FIGURE 3.4

using the given data is shown in figure 3.4a. Notice again that one of the problems is to make sure that the numbers in the table are properly "justified", that is with the hundreds, tens and units in their proper columns. This is another chance to use the PRINT USING statement or you could make use of the program shown in figure 3.4b which allows you to justify numbers since BASIC has this annoying habit of setting numbers into tables with the first digits justified - like this:

```
1235
23
243
4
```

rather than

```
1235
  23
 243
   4
```

which is of far more meaning when totals or averages are required.

V.G.GARAGE GROUP - SALES ANALYSIS

TOTAL SALES   954

YEARLY SALES PER MAN

```
SALESMAN  1   187
SALESMAN  2   168
SALESMAN  3   160
SALESMAN  4    50
SALESMAN  5   192
SALESMAN  6   197
```

AVERAGE MONTHLY SALES

```
SALESMAN  1   15.58
SALESMAN  2   14.00
SALESMAN  3   13.33
SALESMAN  4    4.17
SALESMAN  5   16.00
SALESMAN  6   16.42
```

SALES PER MONTH

	JAN	FEB	MAR	APR	MAY	JUN	JUL	AUG	SEP	OCT	NOV	DEC
SALESMAN NO: 1	13	23	14	11	16	17	18	12	13	19	10	21
SALESMAN NO: 2	3	6	8	19	21	20	12	13	15	16	17	18
SALESMAN NO: 3	12	10	13	13	15	17	18	1	13	14	16	18
SALESMAN NO: 4	5	6	7	8	3	2	5	4	0	2	1	7
SALESMAN NO: 5	10	19	16	15	14	16	18	18	19	20	17	10
SALESMAN NO: 6	6	7	12	13	15	16	17	18	23	24	25	21

FIGURE 3.4a

```
10 DEF FNA(X)=INT(LOG(ABS(X))/LOG(10))
20 DEF FNB(X)=INT(LOG(.1+ABS(X))/LOG(10))
30 READ X
40 IF X=0 THEN STOP
50 T=10
60 IF ABS(X)<.1 THEN 90
70 PRINT TAB(T-FNA(X));X
80 GOTO 30
90 PRINT TAB(T-FNB(X));X
100 GOTO 30
110 DATA 45.567,23.5,.1,6,567.301,23,.001,1,1245.67907
115 DATA 34.0001,45,2,.2,.02,.002,.0002,.00002
120 DATA 0
```

FIGURE 3.4b

Problem 3.5

Here we have a program which is to calculate and print out an electricity bill. The rules for calculating the size of the bill are that there is a standing charge of £5.50 for each bill and that the first 80 units are charged at 4.2 pence per unit. All units over 80 are charged at a lower rate of 1.1 pence each. There is a charge 15% VAT on each bill. Notice that there is the standing charge made even though no electricity has been used. If an obvious error has been made in the reading of the meter then a zero charge is made and the bill would have to be recalculated using the correct figures at a later date. The error picked up by this program is when the previous reading is higher than the present reading giving rise to a negative amount of electricity having been used. Other errors could be introduced if by accident an extra digit was included in the meter reading producing an abnormally large bill. These must also be dealt with.

Data for this program is shown in figure 3.5 and consists of sets of three numbers which represent the consumer number, the present meter reading and the previous meter reading. A value of -999 for the consumer number is used as a "trigger" to signal the end of the data. The output you should obtain with the data given is shown in figure 3.5a. In case you have no PRINT USING statement you could always use the following formula to round to the nearest whole penny

$$P = INT(P*100+.5)/100$$

where P is the amount in pounds. This would cause a value of P of 34.564 to emerge as 34.56 and one of 45.89734 to become 45.90.

```
310 DATA 2314,1090,1010
320 DATA 3241,2347,2347
330 DATA 4564,2381,2300
340 DATA 6743,4567,5402
350 DATA 3341,1221,1119
360 DATA 8234,7689,6543
370 DATA 1231,1200,1121
380 DATA -999,0,0
```

FIGURE 3.5

ELECTRICITY BILLS

| REF:NO | PRESENT | PREVIOUS | UNITS | CHARGE |
	READINGS		USED	
2314	1090	1010	80	10.19
3241	2347	2347	0	6.33
4564	2381	2300	81	9.24
6743	4567	5402	-835	0.00
3341	1221	1119	102	9.50
8234	7689	6543	1146	22.71
1231	1200	1121	79	10.14

TOTAL BILL 68.10 AVERAGE BILL 9.73

FIGURE 3.5a

Problem 3.6

Here is a problem which involves the production of a bank statement. The bank operates the following scales of charges:

(a) Accounts in credit

Current balance	Cost of each transaction
Less than £50.00	10p
Not less than £50.00, but below £100.00	5p
	the balance is never below £100.00 at any time during the year, otherwise 5p.

(b) Accounts overdrawn — Each transaction charged at 15p.

(c) Notes

(1) Charges made annually to customers, charges of 50p or less being waived provided that the customer's account is not overdrawn at the end of the year.
(2) The charge for each transaction is calculated in accordance with the current balance <u>before</u> the transaction takes place (for this purpose an account with a zero balance will be considered as being in credit).

The data for you to try out on your program is shown in figure 3.6. The first number is what is called the "opening balance" and the last credit or debit for the year is followed by a zero entry.

```
250 DATA 52.33
251 DATA 210.32
252 DATA -140.21
253 DATA 10.01
254 DATA -105.28
255 DATA 12.32
256 DATA -50.39
257 DATA 8.62
258 DATA 0.00
```

FIGURE 3.6

The completed statement for the data supplied is shown in figure 3.6a. There are various ways you can approach the problem. You can set up all the output in a table and add new entries to the table as each transaction is processed. There is, however, a problem with this approach in that zero entries in the table will be printed out as zeroes, not as blanks. There are

CITY AND SOUTHERN COUNTIES BANK LTD

	PAYMENTS	RECEIPTS	BALANCE
OPENING BALANCE:			52.33
1		210.32	262.65
2	140.21		122.44
3		10.01	132.45
4	105.28		27.17
5		12.32	39.49
6	50.39		-10.90
7		8.62	-2.28
CHARGES	0.55		-2.83

FIGURE 3.6a

ways round this which will make use of the TAB function in order to get all the credits in one column and all the debits in another.

Problem 3.7

This is a problem which is nothing at all to do with numbers. It is purely "non-numerical" computing. It involves the analysis of a piece of English text and printing out the number of times each word occurs, the average length of each word and the average length of each sentence. In addition a word count can be written into the program to find the number of times a particular word occurs in the text. If this is done to long passages of text it provides a very accurate way of identifying the author of the text. The text for you to analyse is shown in figure 3.7 and the output from your program should look as shown in figure 3.7a.

```
34 LINES OF TEXT
246 WORDS
AVERAGE NO OF WORDS PER LINE IS 7
AVERAGE NO OF LETTERS PER WORD IS 5

WORD COUNT ?YES

WORD TO BE SEARCHED FOR ?and

And monarchs to behold the swelling scene!           LINE NO: 4
Assume the port of Mars; and at his heels,           LINE NO: 6
Leash'd in like hounds, should famine, sword and fire LINE NO: 7
And let us, cyphers to this great accompt,           LINE NO: 17
Whose high uprearing and abutting fronts             LINE NO: 21
And make imaginary puissance;                        LINE NO: 25
Carry them here and there; jumping o'er times,       LINE NO: 29

and    OCCURRED  7 TIMES
WORD COUNT ?YES

WORD TO BE SEARCHED FOR ?that

O for a muse of fire, that would ascend              LINE NO: 1
The flat unraised spirits that hath dared            LINE NO: 9
That did affright the air at Agincourt?              LINE NO: 14
Think, when we talk of horses, that you see them     LINE NO: 26
For 'tis your thoughts that now must deck our kings, LINE NO: 28

that  OCCURRED  5 TIMES
WORD COUNT ?no
```

FIGURE 3.7a

```
O for a muse of fire, that would ascend
The brightest heaven of invention,
A kingdom for a stage, princes to act
And monarchs to behold the swelling scene!
Then should the warlike Harry, like himself,
Assume the port of Mars; and at his heels,
Leash'd in like hounds, should famine, sword and fire
Crouch for employment. But pardon, gentles all,
The flat unraised spirits that hath dared
On this unworthy scaffold to bring forth
So great an object: can this cockpit hold
The vasty fields of France? or may we cram
Within this wooden O the very casques
That did affright the air at Agincourt?
O pardon! since a crooked figure may
Attest in little place a million;
And let us, cyphers to this great accompt,
On your imaginary forces work.
Suppose within the girdle of these walls
Are now confined two mighty monarchies,
Whose high uprearing and abutting fronts
The perilous narrow ocean parts asunder:
Piece out our imperfections with your thoughts;
Into a thousand parts divide one man,
And make imaginary puissance;
Think, when we talk of horses, that you see them
Printing their proud hoofs i' the receiving earth;
For 'tis your thoughts that now must deck our kings,
Carry them here and there; jumping o'er times,
Turning the accomplishment of many years
Into an hour-glass: for the which supply,
Admit me Chorus to this history;
Who prologue-like your humble patience pray,
Gently to hear, kindly to judge, our play.
              FIGURE 3.7
```

Problem 3.8

          Another problem using text is to print it in such a way as to have the text "justified" so that the right hand margin is as straight as the left hand margin. This book was written with the aid of a word-processor program which automatically provides text justification. However, it is quite possible to write a BASIC program to do the same thing. Taking the piece of text shown in figure 3.8, which has a ragged right hand margin, write a program which will cause it to be printed out as shown in figure 3.8a. The point to watch is that of getting each line to finish on a word. Unless you have a printer which allows you to vary the spaces between characters by size rather than by number you will have to do this by adjusting the number of spaces left between the words on each line by an averaging process.

The old village of West Twittering stood astride the River Haste ten miles outside the small market town of Hammling Cross. It was dominated by a church dating from the XI Century which by its size indicated that the village had once possessed an importance far in excess of that of today. The sturdy stone cottages once inhabited by generations of farm hands and the cottage weavers who had provided the village with much of its prosperity in the past now had their thatch neatly trimmed and their rough oaken woodwork replaced by whitepainted soft-wood providing weekend rest houses for the work-weary executives from the nearby large towns. During the week the village slept but come Fridays a whole new population took over "their village" and the sole remaining shop did more trade than during the whole of the preceding five days. Nevertheless, the village did in fact benefit from its new population. The only public house managed to survive. In fact the "Three Tuns" had taken on a new lease of life, although the remaining permanent inhabitants took only grudgingly to the transformation of their cosy "local" with its fading prints of long forgotten harvesters and Sunday School outings for pinafored and pigtailed children into a chrome and plastic "Waggoner's Bar" where the landlord addressed everyone as "Squire". Here were the changes brought about by the twentieth century personified, and not always for the best many said.

FIGURE 3.8

The old village of West Twittering stood astride the River Haste ten miles outside the small market town of Hammling Cross. It was dominated by a church dating from the XI Century which by its size indicated that the village had once possessed an importance far in excess of that of today. The sturdy stone cottages once inhabited by generations of farm hands and the cottage weavers who had provided the village with much of its prosperity in the past now had their thatch neatly trimmed and their rough oaken woodwork replaced by whitepainted soft-wood providing weekend rest houses for the work-weary executives from the nearby large towns. During the week the village slept but come Fridays a whole new population took over "their village" and the sole remaining shop did more trade than during the whole of the preceding five days. Nevertheless, the village did in fact benefit from its new population. The only public house managed to survive. In fact the "Three Tuns" had taken on a new lease of life, although the remaining permanent inhabitants took only grudgingly to the transformation of their cosy "local" with its fading prints of long forgotten harvesters and Sunday School outings for pinafored and pigtailed children into a chrome and plastic "Waggoner's Bar" where the landlord addressed everyone as "Squire". Here were the changes brought about by the twentieth century personified, and not always for the best many said.

FIGURE 3.8a

Problem 3.9

A number of readings are taken at one second intervals of time from a Geiger counter that registers the accumulated emission of particles from a radioactive substance, the initial reading being 36753. Subsequent readings are 36755, 36762, 36766, 36777, 36779 and so on.

Write a program to accept as input N successive readings and to calculate the number of particles emitted each second by taking the difference between successive readings and tabulate the number of times that 0,1,2,3 or more than 3 particles per second occur. The number of times 4 or more particles are emitted per second should be combined. The tabulation should take the form of a bar chart using the * character to represent each entry in each group. Use the data shown in figure 3.9 where the first number is the number assigned to N, the number of readings. The output should look as shown in figure 3.9a

```
270 DATA 33
280 DATA 36753,36755,36762,36766,36777,36779,36780,36780,
    36782,36784,36788
290 DATA 36790,36797,36799,36801,36804,36807,36810,36813,
    36815,36815,36818
300 DATA 36820,36821,36823,36827,36828,36831,36833,36835,
36840,36841,36845
```

FIGURE 3.9

```
0 PARTICLES PER SECOND        **
1 PARTICLES PER SECOND        ****
2 PARTICLES PER SECOND        **********
3 PARTICLES PER SECOND        *******
4 PARTICLES PER SECOND        ********
  OR MORE
```

FIGURE 3.9a

Problem 3.10

This problem combines the use of strings with some very simple arithmetic. It concerns the input of a time in twenty-four hour clock notation and the output from the program is the time in words. This means that 1515 becomes "QUARTER PAST THREE". Some typical outputs are shown in figure 3.10. One way you could approach the problem is to use a string containing the words

"ONETWOTHREEFOURFIVESIXSEVENEIGHTNINETENELEVEN......"

and using the access vector method used in example 2.13.

```
?1215
QUARTER PAST TWELVE
?1500
THREE O'CLOCK
?1427
TWENTYSEVEN MINUTES PAST TWO
?1135
TWENTYFIVE TO TWELVE
? 0
```

FIGURE 3.10

A good way to start this program is to set yourself an easier problem in which you input a single digit, say "9", and print the word "NINE" as output. Then expand the program to deal with a two digit number such as "34" and cause it to output the words "THIRTY FOUR". The trick in this case is to split the number into its component digits and deal with each digit separately. In the same way the final version of the program must first of all divide up a time such as 1234 into 12 (hours) and 34 (minutes). Each of these is divided into its equivalent characters. Don't forget that special times have to be treated in special ways so that "1515" is "QUARTER PAST THREE" but 1514 is "FOURTEEN MINUTES PAST THREE". Try and write a program which is as economical as possible and don't try to cheat by having a separate output for each time, e.g.

```
200 IF T=1515 THEN PRINT "QUARTER PAST THREE"
210 IF T=1516 THEN PRINT "SIXTEEN MINUTES PAST THREE"
220 IF T=1517 THEN PRINT "SEVENTEEN MINUTES PAST THREE"
```

That's not playing the game !

Problem 3.11

This is a further refinement of the bar chart program in Problem 3.9. The object is to draw a bar chart representing the frequency of occurrence of a set of numbers, in this example between 1 and 20. The bars are drawn horizontally and each * represents one occurrence of the number as shown in figure 3.11. For convenience the numbers are shown alongside their bar. This program is not very difficult to write, and a good way to do it is to use a list called, for example, A so that A(1) contains the frequency of occurrence of the number 1, A(10) contains the number of occurrences of the number 10 and so on. The rest is then fairly easy since the list can be scanned to tell the program how many *'s to draw.

The problem becomes more complex if we want to have a bar chart with the bars vertical rather than

```
1    *******************************
2    **********************
3    ***********************
4    *****************************
5    ********************************
6    ***********************
7    ******************************
8    *******************
9    ************************
10   ************************
11   **********************************
12   *************************
13   ***********************
14   ****************************
15   ********************
16   **************************
17   ***************************
18   *************************
19   ***************************
20   **********************
```

FIGURE 3.11

```
*                 *
*                 *
*        *        *
*        *        *
*        * *      *
*        * * *    *
*        * * * *      *        * *    *              *
*    * * * * * *      *        * *    *              *
*    * * * * * *      *        * *    *        *     *
* *  * * * * * *      *        * *  * *  *  *  *  *  *
* *  * * * * * * *  * *    *   * *  * *  *  *  *  *  * *
* *  * * * * * * *  * *  * *   * *  * *  *  *  *  *  * *
* *  * * * * * * *  * *  * *   * *  * *  *  *  *  *  * *
* *  * * * * * * *  * *  * *   * *  * *  *  *  *  *  * *
* *  * * * * * * *  * *  * *   * *  * *  *  *  *  *  * *
* *  * * * * * * *  * *  * *   * *  * *  *  *  *  *  * *
* *  * * * * * * *  * *  * *   * *  * *  *  *  *  *  * *
--------------------------------------------------------
1 2  3 4 5 6 7 8 9 10 11 12 13 14 15 16 17 18 19 20
```

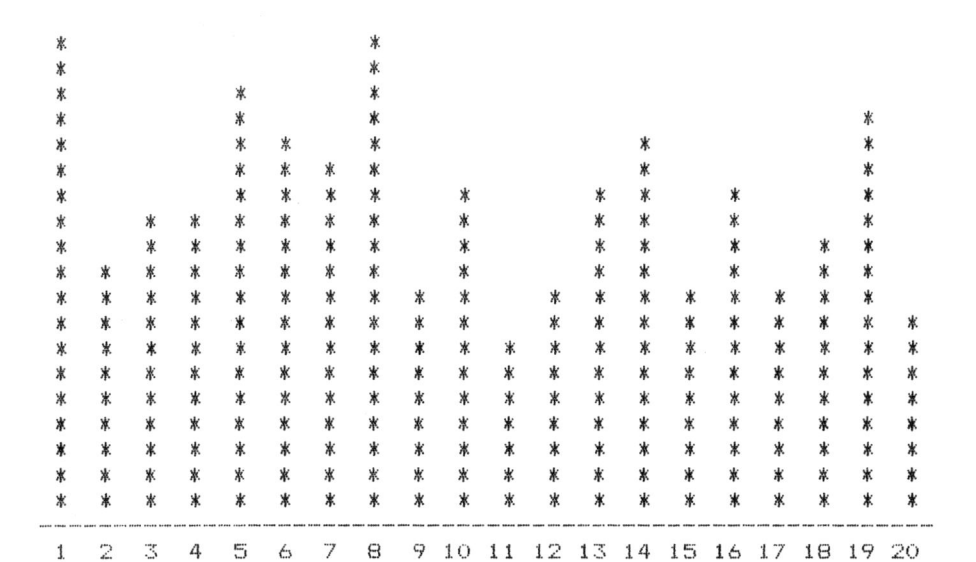

FIGURE 3.11a

horizontal so that the output from the program looks as shown in figure 3.11a. In this case the first thing that has to be done is to consider the screen, or the printer page, as a matrix of "cells" which are to be filled either with *'s or blanks. The table, which must be an array of characters, each of length 1, will then be printed from the top downwards unless the version of BASIC you are using allows you to use graphics commands to draw the bars in. However, in the version of BASIC used for the programs in this book graphics commands are not used and a common subset of the language is used.

4. Real life problems

In this section you will be given a number of real life problems together with the relevant data and some suggestions as to how the problems might be approached. They are really an extension of the examples in the previous section but are more complex in that they need files of data and the programs you write will have to manipulate the data on these files.

Problem 4.1

The first problem concerns a library which needs a computer system to handle its issues and returns. This is only a part of the library's operation but it is one which is ideally suited to computerisation. The crucial file is called the **Master File**. On this file are records containing a reader's name, the book on loan and the date of issue of the book. From this file it is necessary to produce a list of all books overdue, and this has to be done on a daily basis. Also, each day, the master file has to be brought up to date - **updated** - since books are issued and returned each day throughout the day. The returns and new issues are made in a random manner during the day and the data relating to each issue and return - the reader's name, the book title and the date - have to be placed on a file. Before the master file is updated using the data which have come in during the day this data has to have several operations performed on it. First of all the data has to be **validated**. This means that we have to ensure that this new data is suitable for processing. For example, there is little point in processing data relating to a book which does not even exist or a reader who is not registered by the library service. The best way to establish whether or not a book exists is not by means of its title but by means of its ISBN (International Standard Book Number). You will find this number on the book cover and also on the page which contains all the copyright details. This book number is so designed that it is possible to make a very simple arithmetic check to see if the number has been typed in correctly. A program which does this is shown in figure 4.1 and is easily incorporated as a subroutine in any program you may write.

```
1000 INPUT I$
1010 IF LEN(I$)<>10 THEN 1090
1020 T=0:K=10
1030 FOR I=1 TO 10
1040 A=VAL(MID$(I$,I,1))
1050 T=A*K+T
1060 K=K-1
1070 NEXT I
1080 IF T/11 = INT(T/11) THEN 1100
1090 PRINT"ERROR - INVALID ISBN"
1100 STOP
```

FIGURE 4.1

Each book has a unique ISBN which identifies it rather than the title, which could be mis-spelt very easily. For this reason the master file contains the ISBN as well as the book title - see figure 4.1a.

```
0006329497*THE PLANTAGENETS*P.H.MELLORS*050582
0006329500*THE FIRST FOUR GEORGES*S.W.SUMMERS*060582
0090024907*TO GLORY WE STEER*G.KINGHORN*130482
0090037103*FORM LINE OF BATTLE*T.DRAKE*120482
0099055201*ENEMY IN SIGHT!*C.A.WOOD*210482
0099109204*COMMAND A KING'S SHIP*C.HUGHES*140482
0099169703*IN GALLANT COMPANY*H.J.MOON*120482
0140016856*A BREATH OF FRENCH AIR*J.RICHARDSON*200482
0140441719*PASCAL-PENSEES*J.GOSLING*210482
0140442510*BALZAC-LOST ILLUSIONS*C.BRADFORD*220583
0245530312*A GRAMMAR OF PRESENT DAY FRENCH*T.OWEN*230582
0330262726*SMILEY'S PEOPLE*E.R.A.DICK*240582
0330028510*BOMBER*R.A.HARRIS*110582
0333196201*INTRODUCTION TO BASIC*F.JONES*230582
0333253310*FORTRAN FOR STUDENTS*T.THOMAS*220582
0333258258*CODES FOR COMPUTERS*G.MURPHY*050582
0333262867*CONTINUING BASIC*R.SINGH*230582
0333264029*DIGITAL TECHNIQUES*D.HOWARD*110582
0333280792*THE ALIEN,NUMBER EATER AND OTHER PROGRAMS*
          J.RACE*060582
0333286545*PROGRAM YOUR MICROCOMPUTER IN BASIC*R.W.SMITH*
          220582
0333329732*THE SINCLAIR ZX81*R.K.LOOMES*090482
0340198111*HARVEST HOME*J.A.MACINTYRE*190582
0340257334*KANE AND ABEL*K.R.JONES*300582
0435375709*A STUDENT'S GUIDE TO MOLIERE*P.HOOSON*220582
0564003115*GOOD NEWS BIBLE*R.W.A.DICK*290482
0601070569*A BOOK OF BOYS STORIES*P.A.D.SHEEN*120482
0704311402*ALL THE PRESIDENTS MEN*S.WALKER*220582
0708819788*AUTUMN ALLEY*R.C.CLARKE*200582
0931988551*PET/CBM PERSONAL COMPUTER GUIDE*S.L.GREEN*
          240582
2040000305*XVII SIECLE-LES GRANDS AUTEURS*M.P.BARBARY*
          120682
```

FIGURE 4.1a

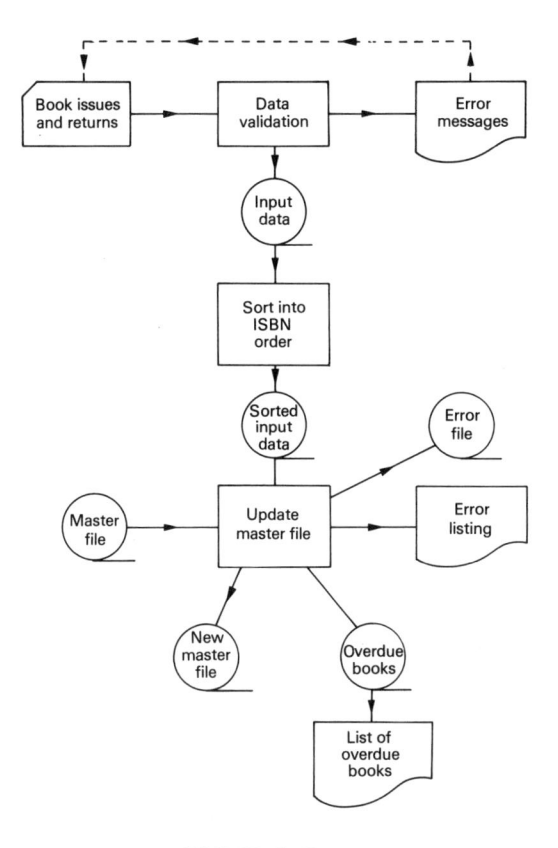

FIGURE 4.1b

The master file is arranged in the order of book titles for ease of searching and so that the input file, which is compiled daily, must end up with its data in the same order as that in the master file. This means that although the data comes in randomly during the day it has to be sorted into book order at the end of the day before the main processing takes place. The sequence of events is shown in figure 4.1b in the form of what is called a **system flowchart.** This shows the sequence of events and the files used by the various programs. The names given to the files are inside the circles and the purpose of each program is shown briefly inside the rectangles. When performing the updating program you must be on the look-out for what are called **reconciliation errors.** These are errors which could occur when, for example, a person returns a book which was not issued in the first place. This sort of error could happen very easily; a library assistant forgets to record the issue of the book or a reader may just take the book from the shelf and forget to take it to the desk. Two days' input are shown in figures 4.1c and 4.1d and these should be dealt with in order by the programs you

26/5/82
0931988691*ISSUE*WORDSTAR MADE EASY*K.POLLARD
0904644707*ISSUE*CREATING SMALL GARDENS*J.GRANT
0333253310*RETURN*T.THOMAS
0140016856*RETURN*J.RICHARDSON
0859390160*ISSUE*PYE BOOK OF AUDIO*J.BORWICK
0851475760*RETURN*E.BOYLE
0850591384*ISSUE*CARING FOR YOUR RENAULT*A.C.WILLIAMS
0564003115*RETURN*R.W.A.DICK
0600362728*ISSUE*ENCYCLOPAEDIA OF MOTOR CYCLES*W.BISHOP
0708819788*RETURN*R.C.CLARKE
0006329497*RETURN*P.H.MELLORS
0335014917*ISSUE*INTRO TO SYSTEMS ANALYSYIS*J.MORGAN
0335014909*ISSUE*PRACTICAL COMPUTER SYSTEMS*J.CHAPMAN
0335014895*ISSUE*COMPUTABILITY*J.CHAPMAN
0335014925*ISSUE*PEOPLE IN THE ELECTRONIC AGE*J.CHAPMAN
0330246631*ISSUE*VET IN HARNESS*J.CRACKNELL
0333253310*ISSUE*FORTRAN FOR STUDENTS*J.WATSON
0931988551*RETURN*L.GREEN

FIGURE 4.1c

26/5/82
0335014925*RETURN*J.CHAPMAN
0564003115*RETURN*R.W.A.DICK
0335014860*ISSUE*CASE STUDIES 1 & 2*J.CHAPMAN
0335041941*ISSUE*CASE STUDY 3*J.CHAPMAN
0330028510*RETURN*R.A.HARRIS
0090037103*RETURN*C.HUGHES
0030492114*RETURN*R.A.BARNARD
0330025031*ISSUE*BELOW STAIRS*L.CRUTCHLEY
0330028677*ISSUE*CLIMBING THE STAIRS*L.CRUTCHLEY
0330029967*ISSUE*FOOTSTEPS OF ANNE FRANK*D.BOND
0340106700*ISSUE*TO ENGLAND WITH LOVE*D.FROST
0330255320*ISSUE*VET IN A SPIN*J.HARDY
0340271590*ISSUE*WHICH ONE'S CLIFF ?*F.SHARMAN
0330246305*ISSUE*THE EAGLE HAS LANDED*P.WALKER
0099097605*ISSUE*GO IN AND SINK!*F.PYM
0330252216*ISSUE*VETS MIGHT FLY*D.ATTENBOROUGH
0330246631*ISSUE*VET IN HARNESS*J.RILEY
0330241567*ISSUE*LET SLEEPING VETS FLY*J.RILEY
0564003115*ISSUE*GOOD NEWS BIBLE*A.ANDREW

FIGURE 4.1d

write. Don't forget to allow for what is called the "end-of-file" condition. In other words, you have to allow for both the following situations: the end of the input file being reached before the end of the master file is reached and the end of the master file being reached before the end of the input file is reached.

This latter situation should not happen, but you should allow for it.

To summarise, your programs should be able to:

(1) validate the input data as it is input to the daily file and print a message such as

>   INVALID BOOK NUMBER - TRY AGAIN

if a mistake is made with the ISBN;

(2) sort the valid data into book title order - i.e. ISBN order once the day's issues and returns have been made;

(3) merge the input file with the master file so that all the new issues are placed on the master file in their proper place and all the returns are deleted from the master file;

(4) detect any reconciliation errors between the new data and the existing data and produce a list of all the input data which causes that type of error;

(5) produce a list of overdue books after the new master file has been created;

Problem 4.2

The next problem is similar to the library problem but is more complex. It deals with an estate agent's business which computerises the filing of houses he has on offer at any time and allows a prospective customer to obtain a list of all the properties which fulfil certain criteria.

The centre of the whole information system is the master file known as **PROP**. For our purposes the estate agent arranges for each property to be identified by a number in the range 0 - 99999 and it is this number which is the "key" to each record and the file is in order of these reference numbers. Each record is divided up into 20 "fields" and each record contains 28 characters as follows:

Field No.	Description	No. of characters
1	Reference no. in range 0 - 99999	5
2	Status: 1 - available 2 - under offer 3 - sold 4 - withdrawn	1

3	Area code 0 -99	2
4	Selling price in thousands 1 - 99	2

5	Town/Country indicator
	    1 - town
	    2 - country
		1

6	Freehold/Leasehold indicator
	    1 - freehold
	    2 - leasehold
		1

7	Type of property
	    1 - house
	    2 - bungalow
	    3 - cottage
		1

8	Nature of property
	    1 - semidetached
	    2 - detached
		1

9	Mains gas
	    1 - yes
	    2 - no
		1

10	Mains electricity
	    1 - yes
	    2 - no
		1

11	Central heating
	    1 - yes
	    2 - no
		1

12	Number of bedrooms 1 - 9	1

13	Garage
	    0 - no
	    1 - single
	    2 - double
		1

14	Number of bathrooms 1 - 3	1

15	Garden
	    0 - none
	    1 - small
	    2 - medium
	    3 - large
		1

16	Vacant possession on completion
	    1 - yes
	    0 - no
		1

17	Currently occupied
	    1 - yes
	    0 - no
		1

18	Telephone currently connected
	    1 - yes
	    0 - no
		1

19	Rateable value in pounds 0 - 999	3

20	Agent has sole selling rights
	    1 - yes
	    0 - no
		1

If there is no entry in the fields numbered 5 to 20 then the information is unspecified.

For example, if one record on the file contained the characters

00147147282121010211310025 01

it would mean that the record referred to property no 00147 (field no 1) which had the following characteristics:

Field no

2	available for sale (1)
3	in area 47 (47)
4	the asking price was £28 000 (28)
5	in the country (2)
6	freehold (1)
7	bungalow (2)
8	detached (1)
9	no mains gas (0)
10	mains electricity (1)
11	no central heating (0)
12	2 bedrooms (2)
13	single garage (1)
14	1 bathroom (1)
15	large garden (3)
16	vacant possession on completion (1)
17	not currently occupied (0)
18	no telephone (0)
19	rateable value £250 (250)
20	agent has sole selling rights (1)

You are provided with two files. One of these is called **PROP** which contains the current master file of all the properties and the other is called **FILE0** which is a file containing all the records which will be used to amend **PROP** and bring it up to date.

VET - this program should validate the data on **FILE0** and produce a validated file of data called **FILE1**.

SORT - this sorts the data on **FILE1** and places it onto a file called **FILE2**.

MERGE - this merges the data on **FILE2** with the existing data on **PROP** to produce a new master file called **FILE3**. Any property which becomes no longer available is placed on a file called **FILE5**.

SELECT - select properties from the master file according to a set of criteria and places them on **FILE4**.

PRINT - prints the contents of any selected file.

The <u>VET</u> program

Each record on the files called **PROP** and **FILE0** consists of a string of 28 characters as described earlier. If fewer than 28 characters have been entered on a record then it is padded out with spaces to make up the 28 characters. If there is any space character in any of the fields then it implies that the characteristic represented by that field is not known. The only fields allowed to have spaces in them are fields 5 to 20. The VET program must check to see if a field contains a non-space character and if it does that it lies within the range specified. In other words, the first field must be a 5-digit number in the range 00000 to 99999, the second field must be a single digit in the range 1 to 4 and so on. Each valid record on **FILE0** must be written to a serial file called **FILE1**.

The <u>SORT</u> program

This program must take the contents of the serial file **FILE1** and sort them into reference number order and the sorted record are to be written to the file called **FILE2**. This could be done by reading the records into a list in memory and performing a sort on this list. A "bubble" sort would do this although it tends to be rather slow. There are other methods which you could investigate which are faster than this type, which is shown in a program in figure 4.2.

```
10 DIM N$(50)
30 READ N
40 FOR I=1 TO N
50 READ N$(I)
60 NEXT I
70 FOR I=1 TO N
80 FOR J= 1 TO N-1
90 IF N$(J)<=N$(J+1) THEN 130
100 A$=N$(J)
110 N$(J)=N$(J+1)
120 N$(J+1)=A$
130 NEXT J
140 NEXT I
150 FOR I=1 TO N
160 PRINT N$(I)
170 NEXT I
180 STOP
190 DATA 20
200 DATA TOM,DICK,HARRY,CHARLIE,FRED
210 DATA TREVOR,CLARENCE,FRANK,EDDIE,DENNIS,ERNIE
220 DATA EDWARD,ROY,PADDY,JOHN,STANLEY,BRIAN
230 DATA MALCOLM,DAVID,BILL
```

FIGURE 4.2

The MERGE program

This program will merge the records held in **FILE2** with the records on **PROP** to form a single serial file called **FILE3**, which is the updated master file. This new master file will of course be the new **PROP** on the next run. If a record on **FILE2** and one on **PROP** are found to have the same reference number then the information on **FILE2** takes precedence and is written to the new file. If, however, there is a field on a record on **FILE2** which is unspecified, i.e. is a blank, then the **PROP** record takes precedence. If field no.2, the status field, contains a 3 or a 4 (sold or withdrawn) on **FILE2** then the record is not written to **FILE3**, the new master file, but is written to a new file, **FILE5** which is the "no longer available" file. Be careful that when you merge the two files there can be reconciliation errors by which the data held on records bearing the same reference numbers fails to match. The vetting program will only pick up obvious errors caused by keying in wrong data which is still apparently valid.

A program which will merge the contents of two files, called "INPUT" and "OLDFILE" is shown in figure 4.2a. The output from the program is shown in figure 4.2b. You can use this program as a basis for your own merging program.

```
10 OPEN "I",1,"B:INPUT"
20 PRINT "CONTENTS OF INPUT FILE"
30 IF EOF(1) THEN 70
40 INPUT#1,A$
50 PRINT A$
60 GOTO 30
70 CLOSE#1
80 PRINT
90 OPEN "I",2,"B:OLDFILE"
100 PRINT "CONTENTS OF OLDFILE"
110 IF EOF(2) THEN 150
120 INPUT#2,A$
130 PRINT A$
140 GOTO 110
150 CLOSE#2
160 PRINT
170 OPEN "I",1,"B:INPUT"
180 OPEN "I",2,"B:OLDFILE"
190 OPEN "O",3,"B:NEWFILE"
200 IF EOF(1) THEN N1$="ZZZZZZ"
210 IF N1$="ZZZZZZ" THEN 230
220 INPUT#1,N1$
230 IF EOF(2) THEN N2$="ZZZZZZ"
240 IF N2$="ZZZZZZ" THEN 260
250 INPUT #2,N2$
260 IF N1$="ZZZZZZ" AND N2$="ZZZZZZ" THEN 380
270 IF N1$<N2$ THEN 310
280 IF N1$=N2$ THEN 350
290 PRINT#3,N2$
300 GOTO 230
310 PRINT#3,N1$
320 IF EOF(1) THEN N1$="ZZZZZZ"
330 IF N1$="ZZZZZZ" THEN 260
340 INPUT#1,N1$
350 GOTO 260
360 PRINT#3,N2$
370 GOTO 200
380 CLOSE#1
390 CLOSE#2
400 CLOSE#3
410 PRINT"CONTENTS OF NEWFILE"
420 PRINT
430 OPEN "I",3,"B:NEWFILE"
440 IF EOF(3) THEN 480
450 INPUT#3,A$
460 PRINT A$
470 GOTO 440
480 CLOSE#3
490 STOP
```

FIGURE 4.2a

CONTENTS OF INPUT FILE
ALBERT
CHARLES
DAVID
EVA
FRANCIS
GEORGE
TREVOR
UNA
VICTOR

CONTENTS OF OLDFILE
ARNOLD
CAROLINE
DENNIS
DONALD
EDWARD
FREDERICK
HAROLD
MAGNUS
TREVOR
VICTOR
WALTER

CONTENTS OF NEWFILE

ALBERT
ARNOLD
CAROLINE
CHARLES
DAVID
DENNIS
DONALD
EDWARD
EVA
FRANCIS
FREDERICK
GEORGE
HAROLD
MAGNUS
TREVOR
UNA
VICTOR
WALTER

FIGURE 4.2b

The SELECT program

This program selects properties from the current master file, according to three criteria. These are input as three numbers. The first of these represents the field which is to provide the selection. The second and third numbers are the range within which the entry will have to lie. For example, if the numbers 4,15,17 are input to this program then details of all properties satisfying the criterion that the price, given in field 4, lies in the range £15 000 to £17 000. An input of 5,1,1 will indicate that field 5, the town/country indicator, must be 1 and 1 only - i.e. a town house. If the field of any property is unspecified then that allows it to be counted for selection. As the selection procedure continues suitable properties are written onto **FILE4**, the selected properties file. Once the selection has been terminated by typing 0,0,0 the last program, the PRINT program can print out details of the selected properties from the file which has been built up during the selection procedure.

The <u>PRINT program</u>

This program will print the contents of any one of the files **PROP**, **FILE3**, **FILE4** or **FILE5**. The raw data held on the file is to be printed out in a form which makes it easy to understand as shown in figure 4.2c.

```
PROPERTY REFERENCE NO: 00021
AVAILABLE
AREA CODE :34
ASKING PRICE IS £34 000
TOWN PROPERTY
FREEHOLD
SEMIDETACHED HOUSE
MAINS GAS
MAINS ELECTRICITY
CENTRAL HEATING
3 BEDROOMS
SINGLE GARAGE
1 BATHROOM
NO GARDEN
VACANT POSSESSION ON COMPLETION
NOT CURRENTLY OCCUPIED
TELEPHONE NOT INSTALLED
RATEABLE VALUE IS £250
AGENT HAS SOLE SELLING RIGHTS



PROPERTY REFERENCE NO: 00022
AVAILABLE
AREA CODE :60
ASKING PRICE IS £33 000
FREEHOLD
DETACHED HOUSE
NO MAINS GAS
MAINS ELECTRICITY
3 BEDROOMS
```

SINGLE GARAGE
1 BATHROOM
NO GARDEN
RATEABLE VALUE IS £266
AGENT HAS NOT SOLE SELLING RIGHTS

PROPERTY REFERENCE NO: 00034
AVAILABLE
AREA CODE :56
ASKING PRICE IS £50 000
COUNTRY PROPERTY
FREEHOLD
DETACHED COTTAGE
NO MAINS GAS
MAINS ELECTRICITY
CENTRAL HEATING
5 BEDROOMS
DOUBLE GARAGE
1 BATHROOM
MEDIUM GARDEN
VACANT POSSESSION ON COMPLETION
CURRENTLY OCCUPIED
TELEPHONE INSTALLED
RATEABLE VALUE IS £345
AGENT HAS SOLE SELLING RIGHTS

PROPERTY REFERENCE NO: 00045
UNDER OFFER
AREA CODE :21
ASKING PRICE IS £15 000
TOWN PROPERTY
LEASEHOLD
SEMIDETACHED HOUSE
MAINS GAS
MAINS ELECTRICITY
CENTRAL HEATING
2 BEDROOMS
NO GARAGE
1 BATHROOM
NO GARDEN
VACANT POSSESSION ON COMPLETION
NOT CURRENTLY OCCUPIED
TELEPHONE NOT INSTALLED
RATEABLE VALUE IS £150
AGENT HAS SOLE SELLING RIGHTS

PROPERTY REFERENCE NO: 00050
UNDER OFFER
AREA CODE :20

ASKING PRICE IS £22 000
FREEHOLD
SEMIDETACHED BUNGALOW
NO MAINS GAS
MAINS ELECTRICITY
CENTRAL HEATING
2 BEDROOMS
NO GARAGE
1 BATHROOM
SMALL GARDEN
RATEABLE VALUE IS £201
AGENT HAS SOLE SELLING RIGHTS

PROPERTY REFERENCE NO: 00055
AVAILABLE
AREA CODE :01
ASKING PRICE IS £66 000
TOWN PROPERTY
FREEHOLD
DETACHED HOUSE
MAINS GAS
MAINS ELECTRICITY
CENTRAL HEATING
4 BEDROOMS
DOUBLE GARAGE
2 BATHROOMS
SMALL GARDEN
VACANT POSSESSION ON COMPLETION
CURRENTLY OCCUPIED
TELEPHONE INSTALLED
RATEABLE VALUE IS £560
AGENT HAS SOLE SELLING RIGHTS

PROPERTY REFERENCE NO: 00056
AVAILABLE
AREA CODE :27
ASKING PRICE IS £45 000
COUNTRY PROPERTY
FREEHOLD
DETACHED COTTAGE
NO MAINS GAS
MAINS ELECTRICITY
CENTRAL HEATING
6 BEDROOMS
DOUBLE GARAGE
1 BATHROOM
MEDIUM GARDEN
VACANT POSSESSION ON COMPLETION
NOT CURRENTLY OCCUPIED
TELEPHONE NOT INSTALLED
RATEABLE VALUE IS £345
AGENT HAS SOLE SELLING RIGHTS

PROPERTY REFERENCE NO: 00066
AVAILABLE
AREA CODE :13
ASKING PRICE IS £87 000
TOWN PROPERTY
FREEHOLD
DETACHED HOUSE
MAINS GAS
MAINS ELECTRICITY
CENTRAL HEATING
6 BEDROOMS
DOUBLE GARAGE
2 BATHROOMS
MEDIUM GARDEN
VACANT POSSESSION ON COMPLETION
CURRENTLY OCCUPIED
TELEPHONE INSTALLED
RATEABLE VALUE IS £679
AGENT HAS SOLE SELLING RIGHTS

PROPERTY REFERENCE NO: 00070
AVAILABLE
AREA CODE :31
ASKING PRICE IS £21 000
TOWN PROPERTY
FREEHOLD
SEMIDETACHED BUNGALOW
MAINS GAS
MAINS ELECTRICITY
CENTRAL HEATING
2 BEDROOMS
SINGLE GARAGE
1 BATHROOM
NO GARDEN
VACANT POSSESSION ON COMPLETION
CURRENTLY OCCUPIED
TELEPHONE NOT INSTALLED
RATEABLE VALUE IS £235
AGENT HAS NOT SOLE SELLING RIGHTS

PROPERTY REFERENCE NO: 00074
UNDER OFFER
AREA CODE :20
ASKING PRICE IS £46 000
COUNTRY PROPERTY
FREEHOLD
DETACHED HOUSE
NO MAINS GAS
MAINS ELECTRICITY
NO CENTRAL HEATING
4 BEDROOMS

SINGLE GARAGE
RATEABLE VALUE IS £350
AGENT HAS NOT SOLE SELLING RIGHTS

PROPERTY REFERENCE NO: 00088
UNDER OFFER
AREA CODE :21
ASKING PRICE IS £89 000
COUNTRY PROPERTY
FREEHOLD
DETACHED HOUSE
NO MAINS GAS
MAINS ELECTRICITY
CENTRAL HEATING
5 BEDROOMS
SINGLE GARAGE
3 BATHROOMS
MEDIUM GARDEN
VACANT POSSESSION ON COMPLETION
NOT CURRENTLY OCCUPIED
TELEPHONE INSTALLED
RATEABLE VALUE IS £679
AGENT HAS SOLE SELLING RIGHTS

PROPERTY REFERENCE NO: 00089
AVAILABLE
AREA CODE :37
ASKING PRICE IS £50 000
COUNTRY PROPERTY
FREEHOLD
DETACHED COTTAGE
NO MAINS GAS
MAINS ELECTRICITY
CENTRAL HEATING
5 BEDROOMS
SINGLE GARAGE
3 BATHROOMS
SMALL GARDEN
VACANT POSSESSION ON COMPLETION
NOT CURRENTLY OCCUPIED
TELEPHONE INSTALLED
RATEABLE VALUE IS £455
AGENT HAS SOLE SELLING RIGHTS

PROPERTY REFERENCE NO: 00102
AVAILABLE
AREA CODE :88
ASKING PRICE IS £45 000
3 BEDROOMS

MEDIUM GARDEN
RATEABLE VALUE IS £345
AGENT HAS NOT SOLE SELLING RIGHTS

PROPERTY REFERENCE NO: 00111
AVAILABLE
AREA CODE :34
ASKING PRICE IS £66 000
TOWN PROPERTY
FREEHOLD
DETACHED BUNGALOW
MAINS GAS
MAINS ELECTRICITY
CENTRAL HEATING
4 BEDROOMS
DOUBLE GARAGE
2 BATHROOMS
MEDIUM GARDEN
VACANT POSSESSION ON COMPLETION
CURRENTLY OCCUPIED
TELEPHONE INSTALLED
RATEABLE VALUE IS £569
AGENT HAS SOLE SELLING RIGHTS

PROPERTY REFERENCE NO: 00112
UNDER OFFER
AREA CODE :44
ASKING PRICE IS £42 000
TOWN PROPERTY
FREEHOLD
DETACHED HOUSE
MAINS GAS
MAINS ELECTRICITY
CENTRAL HEATING
3 BEDROOMS
DOUBLE GARAGE
2 BATHROOMS
MEDIUM GARDEN
VACANT POSSESSION ON COMPLETION
CURRENTLY OCCUPIED
TELEPHONE INSTALLED
RATEABLE VALUE IS £348
AGENT HAS SOLE SELLING RIGHTS

PROPERTY REFERENCE NO: 00134
AVAILABLE
AREA CODE :22
ASKING PRICE IS £37 000
HOUSE
NO MAINS GAS

3 BEDROOMS
RATEABLE VALUE IS £357
AGENT HAS NOT SOLE SELLING RIGHTS

PROPERTY REFERENCE NO: 00145
AVAILABLE
AREA CODE :87
ASKING PRICE IS £45 000
HOUSE
NO MAINS GAS
3 BEDROOMS
VACANT POSSESSION ON COMPLETION
RATEABLE VALUE IS £500
AGENT HAS NOT SOLE SELLING RIGHTS

PROPERTY REFERENCE NO: 00150
UNDER OFFER
AREA CODE :77
ASKING PRICE IS £55 000
TOWN PROPERTY
FREEHOLD
DETACHED HOUSE
MAINS GAS
MAINS ELECTRICITY
CENTRAL HEATING
4 BEDROOMS
DOUBLE GARAGE
2 BATHROOMS
NO GARDEN
VACANT POSSESSION ON COMPLETION
CURRENTLY OCCUPIED
TELEPHONE INSTALLED
RATEABLE VALUE IS £689
AGENT HAS SOLE SELLING RIGHTS

PROPERTY REFERENCE NO: 00159
UNDER OFFER
AREA CODE :11
ASKING PRICE IS £43 000
HOUSE
NO MAINS GAS
3 BEDROOMS
TELEPHONE INSTALLED
RATEABLE VALUE IS £459
AGENT HAS NOT SOLE SELLING RIGHTS

PROPERTY REFERENCE NO: 00161
UNDER OFFER
AREA CODE :20
ASKING PRICE IS £55 000
TOWN PROPERTY
FREEHOLD
DETACHED COTTAGE
NO MAINS GAS
MAINS ELECTRICITY
CENTRAL HEATING
2 BEDROOMS
DOUBLE GARAGE
2 BATHROOMS
MEDIUM GARDEN
VACANT POSSESSION ON COMPLETION
CURRENTLY OCCUPIED
TELEPHONE INSTALLED
RATEABLE VALUE IS £234
AGENT HAS SOLE SELLING RIGHTS

PROPERTY REFERENCE NO: 00164
AVAILABLE
AREA CODE :77
ASKING PRICE IS £45 000
COUNTRY PROPERTY
FREEHOLD
DETACHED COTTAGE
NO MAINS GAS
MAINS ELECTRICITY
CENTRAL HEATING
4 BEDROOMS
DOUBLE GARAGE
2 BATHROOMS
MEDIUM GARDEN
VACANT POSSESSION ON COMPLETION
NOT CURRENTLY OCCUPIED
TELEPHONE INSTALLED
RATEABLE VALUE IS £321
AGENT HAS SOLE SELLING RIGHTS

PROPERTY REFERENCE NO: 00166
UNDER OFFER
AREA CODE :65
ASKING PRICE IS £33 000
COUNTRY PROPERTY
BUNGALOW
NO MAINS GAS
3 BEDROOMS
MEDIUM GARDEN
RATEABLE VALUE IS £300
AGENT HAS NOT SOLE SELLING RIGHTS

```
PROPERTY REFERENCE NO: 00180
AVAILABLE
AREA CODE :44
ASKING PRICE IS £55 000
TOWN PROPERTY
LEASEHOLD
DETACHED HOUSE
MAINS GAS
MAINS ELECTRICITY
CENTRAL HEATING
4 BEDROOMS
NO GARAGE
1 BATHROOM
NO  GARDEN
VACANT POSSESSION ON COMPLETION
NOT CURRENTLY OCCUPIED
TELEPHONE NOT INSTALLED
RATEABLE VALUE IS £600
AGENT HAS SOLE SELLING RIGHTS


PROPERTY REFERENCE NO: 00181
AVAILABLE
AREA CODE :99
ASKING PRICE IS £68 000
5 BEDROOMS
MEDIUM GARDEN
RATEABLE VALUE IS £679
AGENT HAS NOT SOLE SELLING RIGHTS


PROPERTY REFERENCE NO: 00190
UNDER OFFER
AREA CODE :34
ASKING PRICE IS £55 000
TOWN PROPERTY
FREEHOLD
SEMIDETACHED HOUSE
MAINS GAS
MAINS ELECTRICITY
CENTRAL HEATING
5 BEDROOMS
SINGLE GARAGE
2 BATHROOMS
NO  GARDEN
VACANT POSSESSION ON COMPLETION
CURRENTLY OCCUPIED
TELEPHONE INSTALLED
RATEABLE VALUE IS £562
AGENT HAS NOT SOLE SELLING RIGHTS
```

```
PROPERTY REFERENCE NO: 00191
AVAILABLE
AREA CODE :76
ASKING PRICE IS £59 000
HOUSE
NO MAINS GAS
3 BEDROOMS
DOUBLE GARAGE
RATEABLE VALUE IS £600
AGENT HAS NOT SOLE SELLING RIGHTS



PROPERTY REFERENCE NO: 00200
AVAILABLE
AREA CODE :33
ASKING PRICE IS £40 000
TOWN PROPERTY
FREEHOLD
DETACHED HOUSE
MAINS GAS
MAINS ELECTRICITY
CENTRAL HEATING
3 BEDROOMS
SINGLE GARAGE
1 BATHROOM
NO  GARDEN
VACANT POSSESSION ON COMPLETION
CURRENTLY OCCUPIED
TELEPHONE INSTALLED
RATEABLE VALUE IS £450
AGENT HAS SOLE SELLING RIGHTS



PROPERTY REFERENCE NO: 00202
AVAILABLE
AREA CODE :19
ASKING PRICE IS £44 000
TOWN PROPERTY
FREEHOLD
SEMIDETACHED HOUSE
MAINS GAS
MAINS ELECTRICITY
CENTRAL HEATING
4 BEDROOMS
SINGLE GARAGE
1 BATHROOM
SMALL GARDEN
VACANT POSSESSION ON COMPLETION
NOT CURRENTLY OCCUPIED
TELEPHONE NOT INSTALLED
RATEABLE VALUE IS £547
AGENT HAS SOLE SELLING RIGHTS
```

FIGURE 4.2c

Figure 4.2d shows the contents of the file **PROP** and figure 4.2e shows the contents of the file **FILE0**.

```
00021134341111112311110002501
00022160033 112 1 3111    266
00034156502132211521311113451
00045221151211112201010001501
00050220022 1212122012    201
00055101661112111142221115601
00056127452132212621310003451
00066113871112111162231116791
00070131211121112211110235
00074220046211 21041     350
00088221892112211513310016791
00089137502132211513210014551
0010218845    1    3   3   345
00111134661122111422311115691
00112244421112111322311113481
00013412237   11   3      357
00014518745   12   3   1  500
00150277551112111422111116891
00015921143   11   3     1459
00016122055113221222231112341
00016417745213221142231013211
00166265332  2    3   3    3000
00180144551212111401110006001
0018119968     2    5   3   679
001902345511111115121115620
00019117659   12   32    600
002001334011121123111111114501
00020211944111111241121005471
```

FIGURE 4.2d

```
0007432046                 1
0006631387                 1
00020115561112111522210017601
0008842046                 1
0020241944                 0
00182144561112111623210016891
0020034243                 1
150377551
00166365331
00162166342132222501310001500
001903345511
```

FIGURE 4.2e

It would be a good idea if you could arrange for the programs to be "menu driven". In other words, the first thing a user would see would be a "menu" of options for him to choose from. Each subprogram could then be selected and on its completion the menu could be returned to. An example of what a menu display could look like is shown in figure 4.2f.

BROWN,SMITH & YOUNGER. ESTATE AGENTS

VET..............................(1)

SORT.............................(2)

MERGE............................(3)

SELECT...........................(4)

PRINT............................(5)

FINISH...........................(6)

Type 1,2,3,4,5,6 for choice of program.

FIGURE 4.2f

Problem 4.3

The third of our problems involves the extraction of data from a file which this time is an extract from the census returns for a small English town in the Midlands in 1841. The whole file contains 6000 records but only a portion of it is given in this exercise. The file itself is shown in figure 4.3. Each record on the file consists of 26 characters and is, in fact, the only information recorded in that first census taken in 1841. The fields in each record are arranged as follows:

FIELD NUMBER	DESCRIPTION	NUMBER OF CHARACTERS
1	Name	15
2	Sex: 1 = male 2 = female	1
3	Age in years Range - 0-99	2
4	Occupation code 010 - 999	3
5	Whether born locally 02 = yes 20 = no	2
6	Sheet number 001 - 120 (The census was written onto numbered census sheets by the census takers)	3

For example the first record on the file is

             BOON   270120200001

which splits up into

FIELD	CHARACTERS	INTERPRETATION
1	BOON	Name
2	2	Female
3	70	Age
4	120	Occupation - Pensioner
5	20	Not born locally
6	001	Details on Census sheet 1

```
BOON         270120200001
BOON         235120200001
RUDD         285120200001
TOMES        275120200001
HINTIN       275120002001
HINTIN       220120002001
WOODCOCK     230120002001
JONES        270120200001
BELLAMY      280120002001
WOOTTON      280120002001
ENGLISH      280120200001
BRIGHT       270120002001
BRISTOW      265120002001
RAWLING      175120200001
RAWLING      275120200001
MUSE         275120002001
WELLS        180120002001
WELLS        270120002001
HILL         280120002001
HILL         145600002001
HILL         230050002001
HILL         200030002001
JARVIS       255503002001
JARVIS       220120002001
JARVIS       215050002001
JARVIS       210030002001
BRAUM        270120002001
WESTON       260120200001
COLLIER      112030002001
SPICER       265120200001
MITCHELL     155621002001
PIX          250120002001
GROCOCK      250120002001
RYCROFT      209030002001
LANDEN       275120002001
```

DESBOROUGH	28012002001
WALKER	27012002001
WALKER	10403002001
GIBBS	27593002001
HUDSON	27593020002
BEAKES	26093002002
COTTON	26093002002
JENKINS	17093020002
JENKINS	27501002002
THOMPSON	27593020002
SIMPKIN	17593002002
SIMPKIN	27001020002
SIMPKIN	21203002002
COWLEY	27093002002
LADDS	27093002002
LADDS	22512002002
LADDS	20003002002
SMART	21303002002
DAVIDSON	27512002002
RAWLINGS	26050320002
RAWLINGS	13050302002
RAWLINGS	22005002002
RAWLINGS	12050302002
HOLMES	15012020002
SPRIGG	13021520002
HUNTER	21580002002
SMEDLEY	14061102002
GREEN	14061020002
GREEN	24062502002
GREEN	21505002002
GREEN	21505002002
GREEN	11404002002
GREEN	21203002002
GREEN	20903002002
JOHN	10803002002
ALICE	20603002002
HARRISON	21580002002
TASSLE	16012020002
TASSLE	27001020002
BRAKES	15561002002
BRAKES	25001002002
BRAKES	20703002002
BRAKES	20503002002
WARREN	11780502002
ANDREW	13532020002
ANDREW	23001020002
JOHNSON	15563320002
SERGEANT	11404002003
SERGEANT	21103002003
SERGEANT	10803002003
SERGEANT	20503002003
RICHARDSON	16025002003
RICHARDSON	25501020003
RICHARDSON	23099002003
SIMMONS	26012020003

```
BECKWITH      21580002003
RICE          23003020003
SNEY          24001002003
SNEY          11203020003
SNEY          20803020003
COOPER        17012020003
COOPER        26501002003
BAKER         13060320003
JOHNSON       25601020003
JOHNSON       13099902003
WHITE         16068002003
BURMAN        25080002003
ROBINSON      11568020003
MANTON        22080002003
BUCKLE        13044020003
BUCKLE        25512020003
JONES         23912020003
SMITH         23080020003
HIBLINS       23080020003
MARTIN        11380520003
STRICKLAND    13062120003
STRICKLAND    23001002003
STRICKLAND    20503002003
WATERFIELD    11562102003
MERRELL       27512020003
SCHICKLE      17512020003
CLARE         28012020003
GRAYHAM       12532020003
GRAYHAM       22001002003
COBLEY        12564120003
COBLEY        13080520003
SERGEANT      13973002003
SERGEANT      24001002003
BAKER         20603002004
BAKER         20403002004
BAKER         10103002004
HUMSWORTH     11564320004
DIXEY         14034202004
DIXEY         24001002004
DIXEY         10103002004
BUTCHER       28512002004
WHITE         12564120004
EMMANUEL      12565702004
SMITH         12064120004
HARRISON      24512002004
HARRISON      12090402004
HARRISON      12062102004
HARRISON      11562102004
HARRISON      21103002004
HARRISON      10503002004
PHILLIPS      10303002004
PHILLIPS      10103002004
ENGLISH       26501002004
PHIPP         12005002004
CORE          16071020004
```

CORE	26501020004
BRIGG	21580020004
COTTON	14003002004
COTTON	23501020004
COTTON	21203002004
COTTON	10903020004
TABOR	13050202004
SMITH	14060402004
WRIGHT	11103002004
CLARK	13032020004
CLARK	23001020004
CLARK	17012020005
CLARK	11604020005
CLARK	10403002005
CLARK	20203002005
CLARK	10103002005
BUCKY	21203020005
RICHARDS	13560402005
RICHARDS	23501020005
RICHARDS	11003002005
WHALEY	21580020005
BENN	14032020005
BENN	25001020005
BENN	11303002005
BENN	21103002005
SLIM	13034220005
SLIM	22501020005
SLIM	10303020005
CHAPMAN	22562220005
CARNEL	15040020005
CARNEL	24501020005
CARNEL	11562102005
CARNEL	11468002005
CARNEL	20803002005
WILKINSON	17540020005
WILKINSON	25501020005
WILKINSON	11540002005
BRISTOW	24024020005
BRISTOW	12064102005
BRISTOW	21303002005
BRISTOW	21103002005
BRISTOW	20903002005
STEEL	14004002005
STEEL	23501002005
STEEL	21505002005
STEEL	21303002005
STEEL	20803002005
CRISP	14044002005
CRISP	24001020005
CRISP	21505002005
CRISP	11303002005
CRISP	21203002005
CRISP	21003002005
CRISP	20803002005
CRISP	20603002005

CRISP	20403002005
SPRIGGE	21505002005
WIGGEN	15523020005
WIGGEN	25501020006
BRITTAIN	22080002006
BRITTAIN	21580002006
PHERSONS	16563002006
PHERSONS	26501002006
SHEARMAN	11003002005
BANNISTER	24012020006
BANNISTER	21203020006
ROWE	22562220006
RODGERS	12063020006
PHIPPS	13063002006
GIBBS	14063320006
GIBBS	23501020006
GIBBS	21505020006
BURGESS	12564320006
BURGESS	22001020006
BURGESS	10103020006
PARNELL	12064020006
STEPHENS	12064320006
SHAW	16090102006
SHAW	25501002006
SHAW	22262202006
SHAW	21580002006
WALDFOGEL	13065620006
KELLY	11404002006
KELLY	10603002006
SMITH	13062120006
VANDESAM	26224002006
TOW	20403002006
TOW	20303002006
FLETCHER	12046520006
FLETCHER	22001020006
GLOVER	13562120006
GLOVER	20503002006
GLOVER	20103002006
MUNTON	21580002006
HIPPY	25512002006
HIPPY	22062202006
WALKER	13062102006
WALKER	23001020006
BRAY	24012002006
GREEN	12570002006
GREEN	22501020006
GREEN	10203002007
CHRISTOPHER	13532002007
CHRISTOPHER	23501020007
GREY	13562120007
GREY	23501020007
GREY	21405020007
GREY	10803002007
GREY	20203002007
STEVENSON	15063502007

STEVENSON	25001020007
BANNISTER	15060402007
BANNISTER	24501020007
BANNISTER	11560402007
BANNISTER	21505002007
BANNISTER	11504002007
BANNISTER	11303002007
BANNISTER	11203002007
BANNISTER	20503002007
TODD	24050302007
TODD	12050302007
TOOMES	13050302007
FOREMAN	21580002007
GACHES	14030002007
BRODERICK	20503002007
VANDESAM	14024002007
SCOTT	22080020007
TIBBS	15030002007
TIBBS	12012002007
TIBBS	22505002007
FREEMAN	12534220007
NEALS	13034220007
FRIEND	14044120007
HOLMES	23580020007
HOLMES	22080002007
SAUNDERS	22080020007
JENKINS	12032002007
CORE	13030002007
CORE	23501002007
CORE	10903002007
CORE	20703002007
BENNINGTON	22080002007
BURRUS	22080020007
BARLEY	16580502007
DAVIS	13544120007
DESBOROUGH	12080502007
ELLIOTT	23580020008
JOHNSON	21580002008
SPALL	22080020008
WATSON	12480520008
HERITAGE	13044120008
MILTON	15544120008
MILTON	24501020008
NEWTON	12544120008
NOKES	14044120008

FIGURE 4.3

The file of occupations and the codes used for them is shown in figure 4.3a. This is an alphabetical listing. To sort these into numerical order of the codes is a good exercise in sorting techniques.

ACCOUNTANT, 285
ADULT DEPENDANT, 70

AGRICULTURAL LABOURER, 730
ALMSHOUSE PAUPER, 935
ALMSHOUSE, 930
ARMED FORCES, 910
ARTIST/PAINTER, 670
ATTORNEY, 200
AUCTIONEER, 275
BAKER, 503
BANKER, 280
BARBER, 530
BASKET MAKER, 681
BLACKSMITH, 604
BOAT BUILDER, 637
BRAZIER, 603
BREWERY WORKER, 400
BRICKLAYER, 645
BRICKMAKER, 646
BROKER, 445
BRUSH MAKER, 683
BUILDER, 648
BUTCHER, 502
CARPENTER, 633
CARRIER, 341
CHAIR BOTTOM MAKER, 690
CHANDLER, 521
CHILD UNDER 14 AT HOME, 30
CHIMNEY SWEEP, 533
CHINA/GLASS DEALER, 526
CLERK, 230
CLOCKMAKER, 656
COACH/COACH WHEEL MAKER, 634
COMMERCIAL TRAVELLER, 441
CONFECTIONER, 504
COOPER, 635
CORD MAKER, 611
COUNCIL STAFF, 904
CUTLER, 602
DISPENSARY HOUSEKEEPER, 861
DOCTOR, 210
DOMESTIC COACHMAN, 820
DOMESTIC PORTER, 840
DRAPER, 510
DRESSMAKER, 622
DROVER, 735
DRUGGIST, 523
DYER, 450
ENGRAVER, 655
FARMER, 710
FARRIER/HORSEKEEPER, 320
FELL MONGER, 421
FEMALE SERVANT, 800
FISH MONGER, 505
FURNITURE BROKER, 465
GAMEKEEPER, 740
GAOL, 940

GARDENER/NURSERYMAN, 700
GAS WORKER, 663
GLAZIER, 640
GREENGROCER, 507
GROCER, 500
GUN SMITH, 505
HAIRDRESSER AND WIGS, 531
HAT/BONNET MAKER, 625
HAWKER, 506
HORSEBREAKER, 321
HOSIER, 623
HOSPITAL NURSE, 862
HOUSE OF CORRECTION, 942
HOUSEKEEPER, 810
HOUSEWIFE, 10
INNKEEPER/PUBLICAN, 300
IRON MONGER, 520
ITINERANT/TRAVELLER, 965
JEWELLER, 657
JOBBER, 738
JOINER/CABINET MAKER, 630
LACE DEALER, 511
LACEMAKER, 626
LAND PROFESSION, 270
LAUNDERER, 532
LEATHER CUTTER, 613
LEATHER DEALER, 420
LIME KILN LABOURER, 649
LINEN MAKER, 624
LOCK SMITH, 606
LODGE HOUSE KEEPER, 950
MALE SERVANT, 805
MASON, 643
MAT MAKER, 682
MERCHANT, 440
MILITARY OFFICER, 110
MILKMAN, 508
MILLER, 430
MUSICIAN/ENTERTAINER, 671
NO RECORDED OCCUPATION, 999
NURSE/NANNY, 860
OLDER FEMALE CHILD AT HOME, 50
OLDER MALE CHILD AT HOME, 40
OPTICIAN, 218
ORTHODOX CLERGY, 222
PAINTER/BUILDING, 641
PAPER DEALER, 475
PARASOL MAKER, 685
PATIENT, 936
PAUPER, 960
PENSIONER, 120
PIPE MAKER, 689
PLASTERER, 647
PLUMBER, 644
POLICE, 901

PORTER, 346
POSTAL MANAGEMENT, 331
POSTMAN/POSTBOY, 330
POTTER, 684
POULTERER, 755
PRECIOUS METAL WORKER, 659
PRINTER, 650
ROMAN CATHOLIC CLERGY, 220
ROPE MAKER, 680
SADDLER/HARNESS MAKER, 612
SCHOLAR, 20
SCHOOL MASTER/TEACHER/GOVERNESS, 24
SEDAN CHAIR TRADE, 354
SHEPHERD, 737
SHOE MAKER, 610
SHOPKEEPER, 525
SLATER/TILER, 642
STAGE COACHING, 342
STATIONER, 522
SURGEON, 215
TAILOR/BREECHES MAKER, 621
TAPSTER/WINEMAN, 310
TEA DEALER, 415
TIN SMITH, 601
TOLL COLLECTOR, 355
TRUNK MAKER, 687
TURNER/MILLWRIGHT, 631
UNSPECIFIED LABOURER, 750
UPHOLSTERER, 653
VETERINARY SURGEON, 250
VISITOR, 990
WAGGONER, 343
WATCHMAKER, 654
WATER TRANSPORT, 344
WEAVER, 620
WHEELER/WHEELWRIGHT, 636
WHIP MAKER, 686
WHITE SMITH, 600
WIDOW, 60
WINE/BEER SELLER, 501
WIRE WORKER, 607
WOOD CARVER, 638
WOOL/TEXTILE DEALER, 410
WORKHOUSE, 925

FIGURE 4.3a

Having stored the file of data and the occupations code file onto backing store the programs can be written to find all manner of information from the data file. For example, it would be possible to find and list all those people who followed the trade of butcher; all those children in various age groups, so that information regarding infant mortality could be gained, could be listed; all the agricultural labourers between the ages of 30 and 50 could be listed, and so on. The main program could start with a menu asking what pieces of data were of significance and what ranges the ages should be in for example and whether the sex of the person was relevant. You could write a program which would list all the female inhabitants of the town, together with their occupations, in order of age. Once one has file of data of this type there are many things which can be done with such a file. The amount of information which can be extracted from a file of this type is enormous and it is because of the nature of computers that such information is relatively easy and quick to obtain. To extract such information from the original written files would be prohibitively time-wasting and prone to inaccuracy.

Problem 4.4

We must all now be familiar with mailing lists; we all seem to be on one or another which regularly offer us unrepeatable offers, free gifts or magazine subscriptions. How these lists are obtained in the first place is not relevant to this book, but deciding how they are created, maintained and printed out is a very useful exercise. These operations are what this problem is all about. Creating a file of names and addresses is not very difficult and a program which will do this is quite easily written. A typical name and address file is shown in figure 4.4.
Note each record is divided into six fields allowing for a name, surname first, four address fields and a post-code field. The fields are separated by asterisks and the first field, the name, is to be used as the key to the record. This key is used when the records are sorted into name order and when the records are searched in order to be amended or deleted.
The programs which you need to write are **ADD, AMEND, SORT** and **PRINT**.

The ADD program

This program is used to add new names and addresses to an already existing file. The technique involved in this, if the original file is a serial file, is to copy all the existing records onto a new file and add the new records to this new file. This is because you cannot start by reading a file and when you get to a specific point in the file suddenly switch to writing to it. When all the new records have been added the original file can be deleted and the new file given the name of the original file. This is because the new file is opened in write mode and the original file is opened in read mode and they stay that way all through the addition procedure. This is known as **appending** records to a file.

BROWN,MAJOR H.*3 THE CHALETS*LITTLE CLEY*BLAKENEY*NORFOLK*NR4 5TH
GEORGE,MISS L.K.*34 STATION APPROACHES*SURBITON*SURREY**SR4 2EF
HARRIS,MR & MRS B.J.*THE WHITE HOUSE*12 LEOMINSTER CLOSE*SUTTON*SURREY*SR1 4RF
JONES,MR & MRS R.F.*2 OLD GREAT NORTH ROAD*WANTAFORD*NORTHANTS**PE4 6TH
ROBINSON,MISS R.R.*THE OLD RECTORY*BASTON LANE*FRANTISHAM*SUSSEX*DF3 5TK
THOMAS,MRS J.H.*32 CUMBERLAND HOUSE*BOONGATE*PETERSFIELD*HANTS*PO7 9QQ
WATSON,MRS J.*THE LAURELS*55 MORNINGTON CRESCENT*SOUTHAM*SHROPSHIRE*SL1 3TX
GROVES,MAJOR AND MRS T.F.G.*2 BARRACK LANE*WESTPOOL*CHATHAM*KENT*CT8 9HJ
YEOMANS,MR D.R.*THE ALBANY HOTEL*IMPERIAL ROAD*CHESTERFOLD*WARWICKSHIRE*CH9 1RT
WALLACE,COL & MRS W.H.K.*VIMY RIDGE*23 ALMOND GROVE*WERRINGTON*HANTS*PM7 4DC
BANKS,MR J.J.*ABBEY FARM*STACTON TRESSLE*Nr WENLOCK*SALOP*SL4 3PQ
PORTER,MRS ENID*WALMER LODGE*HOWARDS END*WESTON*ESSEX*CL7 4RL
MARTIN,JOHN D.*WITS END*HARVARD GREEN*SLOUGH*BERKS*SH8 2WS
GODDEN,DR.A.*DEPT OF MATHEMATICS*STANTON COLLEGE OF F.E.*STANTON*HANTS*PO9 1QS
MORDEN,REV.R.T.*ST MARY'S VICARAGE*TOLLGATE*STRATTON-UNDER-EDGE*NORFOLK*NR9 5SC
ALLEN,MR R.C.*CITY & COUNTIES CLUB*2 NORTH STREET*PADWORTH*HUMBERSIDE*HL5 3EF
RICHARDS,MR F.*FLAT 5*WEST BUILDINGS*SOUTH STREET*WARMINGTON*WM4 5JK
PERKINS,LT-CDR A.P.R.*H.M.S. EXCELLENT*PORTSMOUTH*HANTS**PT1 4RG
TROWBRIDGE,MR.C.*THE MACMILLAN PRESS LTD*HOUNDMILLS*BASINGSTOKE*HANTS*RG21 2XS
HAMMOND,WALTER J.*SUNNY VIEW*42 HARVARD CLOSE*WESTBOURNE*SUSSEX*BT2 3ED
GELSTHORPE,DR G.*CAMFORD COTTAGE HOSPITAL*CAMFORD GREEN*CAMFORD*HERTS*HT2 2QA
MEECHAN,HARVEY*44 APSLEY WAY*HERTFORD*HERTS**HT5 3RG
GIORDANO,MR E.*HATHERLEY*12 QUEENS PARK RD*CALFORD*HANTS*RG12 5LP
WIGGIN,MR W.*126 FULBRIDGE ROAD*PETERBOROUGH*CAMBS**PE1 8HJ
DICK,MR E.R.A.*UPHILL*LT CASTERTON RD*STAMFORD*LINCS*PE9 4RW
CLARKE,MR R.C.*68 ROMAN BANK*STAMFORD*LINCS**PE9 2QA
GADDES,MR J.G.*71 HIGHFIELD LANE*HEMEL HEMPSTEAD*HERTS**HH2 9SD
GOSLING,MR P.E.*WINDMILL COTTAGE*TINWELL RD*STAMFORD*LINCS*PE9 2QQ
SWALLOW,M.A.*THE OLD BAKEHOUSE*BRIXWORTH*KETTERING*NORTHANTS*KT7 5RD

FIGURE 4.4

The AMEND program

Very often people's addresses, or even names, change and this means that their record on the mailing list must be altered. In addition it is necessary to be able to delete a complete name and address from the file since you do not want to have a file which contains a lot of out-of-date information in particular, information regarding someone who may have died. There are a large number of ways in which this can be done. The easiest way this can be done is by a simple linear search through the file - i.e. from start to finish - until the name is found and then the amendment can be performed. This again requires two files, an old one and a new updated one, in the same way as the appending program. A linear search, however, is very slow and painful especially if the file is of any size. A much better method for searching a file is by the use of a binary search method, but this requires that the file has to be reorganised into a random access file instead of as a serial file. In order for this to work the records in the file have to be in some sort of order, in our example in name order, and then the file is searched using a method as shown in figure 4.4a. First of all the

```
10  DIM N$(30)
20  FOR I=1 TO 30
30  READ N$(I)
40  NEXT I
50  INPUT A$
60  L=1
70  H=30
80  M=H
90  IF L<=H AND N$(M)<>A$ THEN 110
100 GOTO 170
110 IF N$(M)>A$ THEN 140
120 L=M+1
130 GOTO 150
140 H=M-1
150 M=INT((H+L)/2)
160 GOTO 90
170 IF N$(M)<>A$ THEN PRINT"NOT FOUND"
180 IF N$(M)<>A$ THEN STOP
190 PRINT N$(M);" FOUND"
200 STOP
210 DATA ADA,ADAM,BERT,CHARLES,CLARA,CLEONE,DAVID,DIANA,
    DENNIS,DORA
220 DATA EDNA,EDWARD,ERIC,ERICA,ERNEST,FIONA,FRED,GEORGE,
    GREGORY,HAROLD
230 DATA IAN,IVAN,JOHN,JONATHON,KEITH,KEVIN,MARVIN,NORMAN,
    OSWALD,STANLEY
```

FIGURE 4.4a

MISS L.K. GEORGE
34 STATION APPROACHES
SURBITON
SURREY

SR4 2EF

MISS R.R. ROBINSON
THE OLD RECTORY
BASTON LANE
FRANTISHAM
SUSSEX
DF3 6TK

MAJOR AND MRS T.F.G. GROVES
2 BARRACK LANE
WESTPOOL
CHATHAM
KENT
CT8 9HJ

MR J.J. BANKS
ABBEY FARM
STACTON TRESSLE
Nr WENLOCK
SALOP
SL4 3PQ

DR.A. GODDEN
DEPT OF MATHEMATICS
STANTON COLLEGE OF F.E.
STANTON
HANTS
PO9 1QS

MR & MRS B.J. HARRIS
THE WHITE HOUSE
12 LEOMINSTER CLOSE
SUTTON
SURREY
SR1 4RF

MRS J.H. THOMAS
32 CUMBERLAND HOUSE
BOONGATE
PETERSFIELD
HANTS
PO7 9QQ

MR D.R. YEOMANS
THE ALBANY HOTEL
IMPERIAL ROAD
CHESTERFOLD
WARWICKSHIRE
CH9 1RT

MRS ENID PORTER
WALMER LODGE
HOWARDS END
WESTON
ESSEX
CL7 4RL

REV.R.T. MORDEN
ST MARY'S VICARAGE
TOLLGATE
STRATTON-UNDER-EDGE
NORFOLK
NR9 5SC

MAJOR H. BROWN
3 THE CHALETS
LITTLE CLEY
BLAKENEY
NORFOLK
NR4 5TH

MR & MRS R.F. JONES
2 OLD GREAT NORTH ROAD
WANTAFORD
NORTHANTS

PE4 6TH

MRS J. WATSON
THE LAURELS
55 MORNINGTON CRESCENT
SOUTHAM
SHROPSHIRE
SL1 3TX

COL & MRS W.H.K. WALLACE
VIMY RIDGE
23 ALMOND GROVE
WERRINGTON
HANTS
PM7 4DC

JOHN D. MARTIN
WITS END
HARVARD GREEN
SLOUGH
BERKS
SH8 2WS

MR R.C. ALLEN
CITY & COUNTIES CLUB
2 NORTH STREET
PADWORTH
HUMBERSIDE
HL6 3EF

MR F. RICHARDS
FLAT 5
WEST BUILDINGS
SOUTH STREET
WARMINGTON
WM4 5JK

LT-CDR A.P.R. PERKINS
H.M.S.EXCELLENT
PORTSMOUTH
HANTS

PT1 4RG

MR.C. TROWBRIDGE
THE MACMILLAN PRESS LTD
HOUNDMILLS
BASINGSTOKE
HANTS
RG21 2XS

WALTER J. HAMMOND
SUNNY VIEW
42 HARVARD CLOSE
WESTBOURNE
SUSSEX
BT2 3ED

DR G. GELSTHORPE
CAMFORD COTTAGE HOSPITAL
CAMFORD GREEN
CAMFORD
HERTS
HT2 20A

HARVEY MEECHAN
44 APSLEY WAY
HERTFORD
HERTS

HT5 3RG

MR E. GIORDANO
HATHERLEY
12 QUEENS PARK RD
CALFORD
HANTS
RG12 5LP

MR W. WIGGIN
126 FULBRIDGE ROAD
PETERBOROUGH
CAMBS

PE1 8HJ

MR E.R.A. DICK
UPHILL
LT CASTERTON RD
STAMFORD
LINCS
PE9 4RW

MR R.C. CLARKE
68 ROMAN BANK
STAMFORD
LINCS

PE9 20A

MR J.G. GADDES
71 HIGHFIELD LANE
HEMEL HEMPSTEAD
HERTS

HH2 9SD

MR E.R.A. DICK
UPHILL
LT CASTERTON RD
STAMFORD
LINCS
PE9 4RW

MR R.C. CLARKE
68 ROMAN BANK
STAMFORD
LINCS

PE9 20A

MR J.G. GADDES
71 HIGHFIELD LANE
HEMEL HEMPSTEAD
HERTS

HH2 9SD

FIGURE 4.4b

MR R.C. ALLEN
CITY & COUNTIES CLUB
2 NORTH STREET
PADWORTH
HUMBERSIDE
HL6 3EF

MR R.C. CLARKE
68 ROMAN BANK
STAMFORD
LINCS
PE9 2QA

DR G. GELSTHORPE
CAMFORD COTTAGE HOSPITAL
CAMFORD GREEN
CAMFORD
HERTS
HT2 2QA

DR.A. GODDEN
DEPT OF MATHEMATICS
STANTON COLLEGE OF F.E.
STANTON
HANTS
PO9 1QS

WALTER J. HAMMOND
SUNNY VIEW
42 HARVARD CLOSE
WESTBOURNE
SUSSEX
BT2 3ED

MR J.J. BANKS
ABBEY FARM
STACTON TRESSLE
Nr WENLOCK
SALOP
SL4 3PQ

MR E.R.A. DICK
UPHILL
LT CASTERTON RD
STAMFORD
LINCS
PE9 4RW

MISS L.K. GEORGE
34 STATION APPROACHES
SURBITON
SURREY
SR4 2EF

MR P.E. GOSLING
WINDMILL COTTAGE
TINWELL RD
STAMFORD
LINCS
PE9 2QQ

MR & MRS B.J. HARRIS
THE WHITE HOUSE
12 LEOMINSTER CLOSE
SUTTON
SURREY
SR1 4RF

MAJOR H. BROWN
3 THE CHALETS
LITTLE CLEY
BLAKENEY
NORFOLK
NR4 5TH

MR J.G. GADDES
71 HIGHFIELD LANE
HEMEL HEMPSTEAD
HERTS
HH2 9SD

MR E. GIORDANO
HATHERLEY
12 QUEENS PARK RD
CALFORD
HANTS
RG12 5LP

MAJOR AND MRS T.F.G. GROVES
2 BARRACK LANE
WESTPOOL
CHATHAM
KENT
CT8 9HJ

MR & MRS R.F. JONES
2 OLD GREAT NORTH ROAD
WANTAFORD
NORTHANTS
PE4 6TH

90

```
JOHN D. MARTIN              HARVEY MEECHAN              REV.R.T. MORDEN
WITS END                    44 APSLEY WAY               ST MARY'S VICARAGE
HARVARD GREEN               HERTFORD                    TOLLGATE
SLOUGH                      HERTS                       STRATTON-UNDER-EDGE
BERKS                                                   NORFOLK
SH8 2WS                     HT5 3RG                     NR9 5SC

LT-CDR A.P.R. PERKINS       MRS ENID PORTER             MR F. RICHARDS
H.M.S.EXCELLENT             WALMER LODGE                FLAT 5
PORTSMOUTH                  HOWARDS END                 WEST BUILDINGS
HANTS                       WESTON                      SOUTH STREET
                            ESSEX                       WARMINGTON
PT1 4RG                     CL7 4RL                     WM4 5JK

MISS R.R. ROBINSON          M.A. SWALLOW                MRS J.H. THOMAS
THE OLD RECTORY             THE OLD BAKEHOUSE           32 CUMBERLAND HOUSE
BASTON LANE                 BRIXWORTH                   BOONGATE
FRANTISHAM                  KETTERING                   PETERSFIELD
SUSSEX                      NORTHANTS                   HANTS
DF3 6TK                     KT7 5RD                     PO7 9QQ

MR.C. TROWBRIDGE            COL & MRS W.H.K. WALLACE    MRS J. WATSON
THE MACMILLAN PRESS LTD     VIMY RIDGE                  THE LAURELS
HOUNDMILLS                  23 ALMOND GROVE             55 MORNINGTON CRESCENT
BASINGSTOKE                 WERRINGTON                  SOUTHAM
HANTS                       HANTS                       SHROPSHIRE
RG21 2XS                    PM7 4DC                     SL1 3TX

MR.C. TROWBRIDGE            COL & MRS W.H.K. WALLACE    MRS J. WATSON
THE MACMILLAN PRESS LTD     VIMY RIDGE                  THE LAURELS
HOUNDMILLS                  23 ALMOND GROVE             55 MORNINGTON CRESCENT
BASINGSTOKE                 WERRINGTON                  SOUTHAM
HANTS                       HANTS                       SHROPSHIRE
RG21 2XS                    PM7 4DC                     SL1 3TX
```

FIGURE 4.4c

middle record of the file has to be found and we decide if the record we wish to amend lies before or after the middle record. After this has been established then we can divide the "target" half of the file into two again and discover which half now contains the record we want. This is then continued until the required record is finally located. This can only be done on a random or direct access file where we can write to or read from any record at will.

The PRINT program

The PRINT program should read the names and addresses from the file and print them out, preferably on sticky labels which can usually be bought in rolls the same width, or smaller, as the paper which is used in a printer. The printed names and addresses can then be peeled off and fixed onto envelopes. Such sticky labels can be obtained in single width, two labels across, three labels across or four labels across. If, as in the result shown in figure 4.4b, we print three addresses across the width then a certain amount of skill has to be used in making sure that the right address is allocated to each name. Also there are problems if the number of names printed is not an exact multiple of three.

The SORT program

In order to ensure that we get no repeated names, or repeated addresses on our file, we really should sort it into name order. This ensures that we do not send two letters to the same person or more than one letter to each house, unless there is a good reason for doing so. For example, three people in one house may all want bank statements sent to them individually, but a circular really only needs to be sent one to each house. Sorting records on a file is quite complicated if it is to be efficient and there are basically two ways in which it can be done. The first of these, and the most time-consuming, is to read all the records in the file into a list in memory and then sort them using any of the standard methods of sorting lists. This is usually known as an **in-core** sorting method and for large files requires the computer to have a very large amount of memory available. If the sorting is to be performed on the records themselves there are a number of methods ranging from the so-called **polyphase** sort which is described in "Continuing BASIC" - P.E.Gosling, Macmillan (Chapter 5),which uses serial files to a simple variation on the bubble sort program which uses random files. The result of sorting the file of names and addresses is shown in figure 4.4c.

5. Using random access files

The final section of this book gives you a start in the use of random, or direct, access files. The important feature that these files have that serial files do not is that any record in the file can be read from or written to directly and without reference to any other records in the file. Once the file has been opened we can access any record for reading or writing without any change in mode. To open a random file we have to use the instruction

                OPEN "R",fn,"FILENAME"

where fn is the logical number of the file within that program. Each record on the file is allowed to be up to 128 bytes in length and each record can only contain string data. This means that each record can contain up to 128 characters. We define the length and contents of each "field" within each record by means of a FIELD instruction of which the following is an example:

                FIELD 1,20 AS A$,12 AS B$,10 AS C$

which states that each record of file number 1 contains three fields, the first called A$ occupies 20 bytes, the next is called B$ and contains 12 bytes and the third called C$ is 10 bytes long. This means that a total of 42 out of the available 128 bytes are used. There are ways of using up the space more efficiently, but more of that later.

       What the FIELD instruction does is to define an area in memory called a **buffer** and the data to be placed into each record has to be loaded into that buffer before being written to the record. In other words, it is the contents of the buffer which are placed in a record using a PUT instruction. For this we write

                PUT 1,R

which is the instruction to place the contents of the buffer into record number R in file number 1. However, before we can **PUT** anything into a record we have to ensure that all the data has been formatted properly and converted into string data. For example we might want to place three items of data, called X$,Y and Z into a record of file number 1, as specified in field description earlier on this page. For this purpose we have five instructions available. These are LSET,RSET,MKI$,MKS$ and MKD$.

- LSET - places a string at the left hand end of the field.
- RSET - places a string at the right hand end of the field.
- MKI$ - converts a number into a 2-byte integer string.
- MKS$ - converts a number into a 4-byte single precision string.
- MKD$ - converts a number into an 8-byte double precision string.

The sequence involved in writing of the three pieces of data would be first to open the file and define its file number and name

```
OPEN "R",1,"DATAFILE"
```

then to define the fields within a record

```
FIELD 1,10 AS A$,2 AS B$,4 AS C$
```

then we input the data

```
INPUT X$,Y%,Z
```

then we place the data into the buffer

```
LSET A$=X$
LSET B$=MKI$(Y%)
LSET C$=MKS$(Z)
```

and we then place the contents of the buffer into a specified record in the file; in this case record number 10;

```
PUT 1,10
```

Having placed a record on a file we need to be able to read it back in order to do things with the data it contains. This time the keyword is **GET** and to read the contents of record number 10 into the buffer from the disc where it is stored we would write

```
GET 1,10
```

If we had kept the same field definition as previously used we would now have three strings in the buffer and they are called A$, B$ and C$. A$ was a string anyway, so we have no problems with that. However, B$ and C$ have to be converted back into numbers and for this purpose we use

CVI - converts a string into an integer.

CVS - converts a string into a single precision number.

CVD - converts a string into a double precision number.

We then can write

$$X\% = CVI(B\$)$$
$$Z = CVS(C\$)$$

which will convert the string B$ into an integer number X% and the string C$ into the single precision number Z.

A simple example of the use of random access files is in the example program shown in figure 5.1.

```
10 OPEN "R",1,"TELEPHONE"
20 FIELD 1,20 AS F1$,20 AS F2$
30 J=50
40 K=0
50 J=J-1
60 FOR I=1 TO J
70 GET 1,I:A1$=F1$:A2$=F2$
80 GET 1,I+1:B1$=F1$:B2$=F2$
90 IF A2$>B2$ THEN 130
100 NEXT I
110 IF K=0 THEN 190
120 GOTO 40
130 LSET F1$=B1$:LSET F2$= B2$
140 PUT 1,I
150 LSET F1$=A1$:LSET F2$=A2$
160 PUT 1,I+1
170 K=1
180 GOTO 100
190 FOR I=1 TO 50
200 GET 1,I
210 PRINT F1$;": ";F2$
220 NEXT I
230 STOP
240 CLOSE 1
```

FIGURE 5.1

```
L AND J              : 01-204 7525
COMPUTEACH           : 01-388 0691
COMPUTEACH           : 01-388 0692
LANDSOFT             : 01-549 1178
ADDA                 : 01-579 5845
MEDICOM              : 01-579 5845
CETRONIC             : 01-581 1011
NCR                  : 01-638 6200
OFFICE-MATE          : 01-878 7044
WILKES               : 01-900 0471
STAGE ONE            : 0202-295395
B & B                : 0204-26644
DATAVIEW             : 0206-865835
MICRO ASSOC.         : 021-328 4574
MIDLANDS C.S.        : 021-382 4171
A.C.T.               : 021-454 8585
RADAN                : 0225-318483
CORTEX               : 0234-213571
MMS                  : 0234-40601
BRHA                 : 0234-750422
UPTHORPE             : 0235-850747
MACMILLAN            : 0256-29242
GATE M.S.            : 0382-28194
PRENTICE-HALL        : 0442-58531
COMPSOFT             : 0483-39665
DALATLECT            : 04862-25995
TAYLOR WILSON        : 05645-6192
MILLS ASS.           : 0600-4611
NCC                  : 061-228 6333
COMPUTASTORE         : 061-832 4761
SUMLOCK              : 061-834 4233
CYTEK                : 061-872 4682
I.C.I.               : 0642-553601
IJJ DESIGN           : 0672-54487
CLAREMONT CONTROLS   : 0699-21081
PROF.SOFTWARE        : 0707-42184
KINGSTON             : 0723-514141
AUTOMATION           : 073-522 3012
ARDEN D.P.           : 0733-47767
PETERBOROUGH TECH.   : 0733-67366
AUDIOGENIC LTD       : 0734-595269
COMMODORE            : 0753-79292
STAMFORD COLLEGE     : 0780-4141
WEGO COMPUTERS       : 0883-49235
JCL SOFTWARE         : 0892-27454
TIRTH LTD            : 0908-679528
MACHSIZE             : 0926-312542
CHARLIE              : 3421
HARRY                : 5643
GEORGE               : 7658
```

FIGURE 5.1a

A.C.T.	021-454 8585
ADDA	01-579 5845
ARDEN D.P.	0733-47767
AUDIOGENIC LTD	0734-595269
AUTOMATION	073-522 3012
B & B	0204-26644
BRHA	0234-750422
CETRONIC	01-581 1011
CHARLIE	3421
CLAREMONT CONTROLS	0699-21081
COMMODORE	0753-79292
COMPSOFT	0483-39665
COMPUTASTORE	061-832 4761
COMPUTEACH	01-388 0692
COMPUTEACH	01-388 0691
CORTEX	0234-213571
CYTEK	061-872 4682
DALATLECT	04862-25995
DATAVIEW	0206-865835
GATE M.S.	0382-28194
GEORGE	7658
HARRY	5643
I.C.I.	0642-553601
IJJ DESIGN	0672-54487
JCL SOFTWARE	0892-27454
KINGSTON	0723-514141
L AND J	01-204 7525
LANDSOFT	01-549 1178
MACHSIZE	0926-312542
MACMILLAN	0256-29242
MEDICOM	01-579 5845
MICRO ASSOC.	021-328 4574
MIDLANDS C.S.	021-382 4171
MILLS ASS.	0600-4611
MMS	0234-40601
NCC	061-228 6333
NCR	01-638 6200
OFFICE-MATE	01-878 7044
PETERBOROUGH TECH.	0733-67366
PRENTICE-HALL	0442-58531
PROF.SOFTWARE	0707-42184
RADAN	0225-318483
STAGE ONE	0202-295395
STAMFORD COLLEGE	0780-4141
SUMLOCK	061-834 4233
TAYLOR WILSON	05645-6192
TIRTH LTD	0908-679528
UPTHORPE	0235-850747
WEGO COMPUTERS	0883-49235
WILKES	01-900 0471

FIGURE 5.1b

This uses an extension of the bubble sort program shown in figure 4.2. That was an example of the sorting being performed in the RAM of the computer. The example shown here is of the same operation being made on a series of names and telephone numbers stored in a random access file called "TELEPHONE". The names and numbers were placed in successive records of the file in no particular order and the program listed sorts them into order of telephone number and then prints out the final ordered list as shown in figure 5.1a. Note that instead of the swapping routine in lines 100-120 of figure 4.2 the program shown in figure 5.1 merely writes the records which were not in the correct order back into the opposite records - lines 130-160.

A program which was used to sort the records - note that in these examples the actual records are moved about and swapped over - into alphabetical order of names as shown in figure 5.1b and the program used to do it is listed in figure 5.1c.

```
10 OPEN "R",1,"TELEPHONE"
20 FIELD 1,20 AS F1$,20 AS F2$
30 M=50
40 M=INT(M/2)
50 IF M<=0 THEN 240
60 K=50-M
70 J=1
80 I=J
90 R=I+M
100 GET 1,I
110 A1$=F1$:A2$=F2$
120 GET 1,R
130 B1$=F1$:B2$=F2$
140 IF A1$<=B1$ THEN 210
150 LSET F1$=B1$:LSET F2$=B2$
160 PUT 1,I
170 LSET F1$=A1$:LSET F2$=A2$
180 PUT 1,R
190 I=I-M
200 IF I>0 THEN 90
210 J=J+1
220 IF J<=K THEN 80
230 GOTO 40
240 FOR I= 1 TO 50
250 GET 1,I
260 PRINT F1$,F2$
270 NEXT I
```

FIGURE 5.1c

This method is faster, but much more difficult to explain why, than a bubble sort. It is called a **shell** sort. Note, however, that methods of sorting on backing store, discs, are slower than methods where the sorting is done in RAM. They are useful if memory is at a premium and very often sorted files are essential anyway. There are other methods of sorting of which one, the polyphase sort mentioned in the previous chapter, sorts serial files by a series of mergers of two files into one. The most efficient sorting methods are often based on serial files as it turns out. Nevertheless random files are of great importance because although they may not allow us to sort very quickly it is possible to use them in such a way that the sorting is done for us as the data is loaded into the file. For this purpose we deliberately structure our files so that even though the data is presented to the file in a random order the data is placed in the records in such a way as to construct an order as we go along. This uses the technique known as a **linked list**. In this the records not only contain the data we are interested in but also a field in each record contains a link or pointer to the next record which is logically in sequence. In our example we shall have a file which contains a series of ten names which are filed in records 1 to 10 as shown in the table below:

Record number	Name	Link to next record
1	GEORGE	8
2	BILL	7
3	FRANCIS	1
4	IVAN	5
5	JOHN	-1
6	DAVID	9
7	CHARLES	6
8	HAROLD	4
9	EVA	3
10	ARTHUR	2

A program which is used to print the contents of the file in order needs to know where to start and the first record in order is number 10. This record has a pointer which tells the program that the next in order is record number 2. Record number 2 points to record number 7, record 7 to record 6 and so on. The last record in the sequence is record number 5 which has -1 as its pointer. This special pointer tells the program that it has reached the last record of the alphabetical sequence. The problem now is twofold. Firstly, how do we add new records to the file and arrange the pointers so that it will still be printed out in sequence ? Secondly, how do we delete a record from the file ? Both of these questions are made easier by the use of a **free storage** list. This consists of a series of blank records which are linked to each other in the same way as the main file. When a record is added to the file it is placed in the first available record in the free storage list and the pointers, not only between the records themselves but also to the heads of both lists, are adjusted. Deletion of a record from the file merely returns the superfluous record from the file to the free storage list and amends the pointers accordingly. A program which prints out the contents of the file and also the free storage list is shown in figure 5.2. The result of running it is shown in figure 5.2a.

```
10  OPEN "R",1,"LINKFL"
20  FIELD 1, 12 AS N$,2 AS L$
30  C=1
40  INPUT "FIRST REC NO:";R
60  GET 1,R
70  C=C+1
80  PRINT"RECORD NO;";R;PRINT TAB(20);N$;"LINK TO NEXT
    RECORD:";CVI(L$)
90  R=CVI(L$)
100 IF R=-1 THEN 120
110 GOTO 60
120 PRINT "HEAD OF FREE STORAGE LIST IS:";C
130 GET 1,C
140 PRINT "RECORD NO:";C;:PRINT TAB(20);"EMPTY :";"LINK
    TO NEXT RECORD:"
150 L=CVI(L$)
160 C=C+1
170 IF L=-1 THEN 190
180 GOTO 130
190 PRINT "END OF FILE"
200 CLOSE
```

FIGURE 5.2

If a new record is added to the file then the contents of the file and its free storage list will become as shown in figure 5.2b. You should be able to write a program which will create a linked list file from scratch, add records to it and delete records from it. Pay particular attention to three points:

(1) Adding a record whose key precedes all the others.
(2) Adding a record which becomes the logically last record in the sequence.
(3) Deleting records which are logically first or last in the sequence.

A logical extension of the hashing procedure can be applied to files. This ensures that if the record number of the data being searched for is dependant on some sort of key then the amount of searching is kept to a minimum. For example, if a file contains 50 records of names and telephone numbers, all of which are simple four-digit numbers, then it is possible to allocate each record of name and number

```
FIRST RECORD NO: ? 10
RECORD NO: 10      ARTHUR      LINK TO NEXT RECORD: 2
RECORD NO: 2       BILL        LINK TO NEXT RECORD: 7
RECORD NO: 7       CHARLES     LINK TO NEXT RECORD: 6
RECORD NO: 6       DAVID       LINK TO NEXT RECORD: 9
RECORD NO: 9       EVA         LINK TO NEXT RECORD: 3
RECORD NO: 3       FRANCIS     LINK TO NEXT RECORD: 1
RECORD NO: 1       GEORGE      LINK TO NEXT RECORD: 8
RECORD NO: 8       HAROLD      LINK TO NEXT RECORD: 4
RECORD NO: 4       IVAN        LINK TO NEXT RECORD: 5
RECORD NO: 5       JOHN        LINK TO NEXT RECORD:-1
HEAD OF FREE STORAGE LIST IS: 11
RECORD NO: 11      EMPTY :LINK TO NEXT RECORD: 12
RECORD NO: 12      EMPTY :LINK TO NEXT RECORD: 13
RECORD NO: 13      EMPTY :LINK TO NEXT RECORD: 14
RECORD NO: 14      EMPTY :LINK TO NEXT RECORD: 15
RECORD NO: 15      EMPTY :LINK TO NEXT RECORD: 16
RECORD NO: 16      EMPTY :LINK TO NEXT RECORD: 17
RECORD NO: 17      EMPTY :LINK TO NEXT RECORD: 18
RECORD NO: 18      EMPTY :LINK TO NEXT RECORD: 19
RECORD NO: 19      EMPTY :LINK TO NEXT RECORD: 20
RECORD NO: 20      EMPTY :LINK TO NEXT RECORD: 21
RECORD NO: 21      EMPTY :LINK TO NEXT RECORD: 22
RECORD NO: 22      EMPTY :LINK TO NEXT RECORD: 23
RECORD NO: 23      EMPTY :LINK TO NEXT RECORD: 24
RECORD NO: 24      EMPTY :LINK TO NEXT RECORD: 25
RECORD NO: 25      EMPTY :LINK TO NEXT RECORD: 26
RECORD NO: 26      EMPTY :LINK TO NEXT RECORD: 27
RECORD NO: 27      EMPTY :LINK TO NEXT RECORD: 28
RECORD NO: 28      EMPTY :LINK TO NEXT RECORD: 29
RECORD NO: 29      EMPTY :LINK TO NEXT RECORD: 30
RECORD NO: 30      EMPTY :LINK TO NEXT RECORD:-1
END OF FILE
```

FIGURE 5.2a

with a number found by a simple hashing routine. In our example we shall simply take the first two digits of the number and divide by 2. Then we take the integer part or the result and this gives us a number in which we may find the record. It is possible that the record is already occupied since more than one number wish reduce to one record number. For example, the numbers 4456 and 4567 both reduce to 22. If a record is already occupied by a name and number, then the next in sequence is tried. If that is occupied, then the next is tried. If the 50th record is occupied the search starts again at record number 1. This is how the records are put on the file in the first place and by the same method a particular number is searched for in the file. Figure 5.3 shows the records on the file printed out and you should be able to see how the record numbers and the four figure numbers in the records are related. The program shown in figure 5.3a shows how the searches are made. You should write a program to set up the file in the first place.

```
FIRST RECORD NO: ? 10
RECORD NO: 10       ARTHUR      LINK TO NEXT RECORD: 2
RECORD NO: 2        BILL        LINK TO NEXT RECORD: 7
RECORD NO: 7        CHARLES     LINK TO NEXT RECORD: 6
RECORD NO: 6        DAVID       LINK TO NEXT RECORD: 9
RECORD NO: 9        EVA         LINK TO NEXT RECORD: 3
RECORD NO: 3        FRANCIS     LINK TO NEXT RECORD: 11
RECORD NO: 11       FRED        LINK TO NEXT RECORD: 1
RECORD NO: 1        GEORGE      LINK TO NEXT RECORD: 8
RECORD NO: 8        HAROLD      LINK TO NEXT RECORD: 4
RECORD NO: 4        IVAN        LINK TO NEXT RECORD: 5
RECORD NO: 5        JOHN        LINK TO NEXT RECORD:-1
HEAD OF FREE STORAGE LIST IS: 12
RECORD NO: 12       EMPTY :LINK TO NEXT RECORD: 13
RECORD NO: 13       EMPTY :LINK TO NEXT RECORD: 14
RECORD NO: 14       EMPTY :LINK TO NEXT RECORD: 15
RECORD NO: 15       EMPTY :LINK TO NEXT RECORD: 16
RECORD NO: 16       EMPTY :LINK TO NEXT RECORD: 17
RECORD NO: 17       EMPTY :LINK TO NEXT RECORD: 18
RECORD NO: 18       EMPTY :LINK TO NEXT RECORD: 19
RECORD NO: 19       EMPTY :LINK TO NEXT RECORD: 20
RECORD NO: 20       EMPTY :LINK TO NEXT RECORD: 21
RECORD NO: 21       EMPTY :LINK TO NEXT RECORD: 22
RECORD NO: 22       EMPTY :LINK TO NEXT RECORD: 23
RECORD NO: 23       EMPTY :LINK TO NEXT RECORD: 24
RECORD NO: 24       EMPTY :LINK TO NEXT RECORD: 25
RECORD NO: 25       EMPTY :LINK TO NEXT RECORD: 26
RECORD NO: 26       EMPTY :LINK TO NEXT RECORD: 27
RECORD NO: 27       EMPTY :LINK TO NEXT RECORD: 28
RECORD NO: 28       EMPTY :LINK TO NEXT RECORD: 29
RECORD NO: 29       EMPTY :LINK TO NEXT RECORD: 30
RECORD NO: 30       EMPTY :LINK TO NEXT RECORD:-1
END OF FILE
```

FIGURE 5.2b

```
10 OPEN "R",1,"PHONE"
20 FIELD 1,4 AS N$,10 AS A$
30 INPUT "NO TO BE SEARCHED FOR:";N1$
40 R=0
50 K=VAL( LEFT$(N1$,2))
60 K=INT(K/2)
70 GET 1,K
80 R=R+1
90 IF N$=N1$ THEN 150
100 K=K+1
110 IF R=50 THEN 190
120 IF K=50 THEN LET K=1
130 GOTO 70
140 END
150 PRINT N$,A$
160 INPUT "ANY MORE ";Y$
170 IF Y$="YES" THEN 30
180 STOP
190 PRINT "NUMBER NOT FOUND"
200 GOTO 160
```

FIGURE 5.3a

RECORD NO	NUMBER	NAME
1	9915	CAPES
2	9821	MAYWOOD
3	-999	0
4	-999	0
5	1111	WALL
6	-999	0
7	-999	0
8	-999	0
9	-999	0
10	-999	0
11	2343	SMITH
12	2223	THOMPSON
13	-999	0
14	-999	0
15	-999	0
16	3341	THATCHER
17	3215	HOWES
18	-999	0
19	3962	TAYLOR
20	-999	0
21	-999	0
22	4444	HEALY
23	-999	0
24	-999	0
25	-999	0
26	5252	WOOD
27	5571	WATERMAN
28	-999	0
29	-999	0
30	-999	0
31	-999	0
32	-999	0
33	-999	0
34	-999	0
35	-999	0
36	-999	0
37	-999	0
38	7762	ASH
39	7890	GREEN
40	-999	0
41	-999	0
42	-999	0
43	-999	0
44	8897	SIMPSON
45	9087	EVANS
46	8976	HEATH
47	8875	COON
48	8890	FOOT
49	9901	FINCH
50	9876	BOND

FIGURE 5.3

A useful variation on this theme is to store the file using a key which is based on a hash value derived from the name rather than the number. We would use a simple code in which we consider, say, the first six letters of the surname and assign numerical values to them by a simple code - A=1,B=2,C=3, etc. These numbers could then be added together and reduced by some rule to a number between, in our example, 1 and 50. Then the amount of time spent in searching right through the file from start to finish is greatly reduced. Remember that the records in the file are not ordered in any way so that the only other way would be by a straight linear search which is very time-consuming. A program which will hash code a name of up to six characters and then reduce the resulting number to a number between 1 and 50 is shown in figure 5.3b.

```
10 A$="ABCDEFGHIJKLMNOPQRSTUVWXYZ"
20 INPUT N$
30 T=0
40 FOR I=1 TO 6
50 FOR J=1 TO 26
60 IF MID$(N$,I,1)=MID$(A$,J,1) THEN T=T+J
70 NEXT J
80 NEXT I
90 PRINT T
100 R=T-INT(T/50)*50+1
110 PRINT R
```

FIGURE 5.3b

Now it is fairly obvious that if we are forced to use records which are fixed at a length of 128 bytes we are going to waste space if we are only going to store data which only takes up, say, 25 bytes per record. This problem is fairly easy to overcome if we organise our file so that several records can be stored in each set of 128 bytes. This is done by dividing our records up into a set of "sub-records". For example, if we were intending to store records of the stock held by a company using a random access file we might store two fields relating to each stock item, a description of the stock item and the number held in stock. We use the part number of each stock item to provide us with a key to the record in which the details of that item is kept. In our example we shall use a set of part numbers from 1000 to 9999. We also intend to store the description in a field 21 bytes long and the number in stock in a field 4 bytes long. This means that with 25 bytes available for each record we can store details of five stock items in each record, leaving only 3 bytes wasted. To calculate the record number where the data is stored from the part number itself we use a form of hashing rule as follows:

Record No = INT((Part no -1000)/5) +1

This means that the record number containing details of part number 1000 is INT((1000-1000)/5)+1 = 1. Details of part number 2016 will be found in record number INT((2016-1000)/5)+1 = 204.
Each of our records will contain five sub-records and the sub-record number is found as follows:

Sub-record No = Part no - (Record No -1)*5 - 999

so that the record for part number 1000 is found in sub-record 1000 - (1-1)*5 - 999 = 1 of record 1, whereas the record for part number 1001 is found in sub-record 1001 - (1-1)*5 - 999 = 2 of record number 1. The record for part number 1083 is to be found in sub-record 4 of record 17. In the example shown in figure 5.4 we use a variable field statement to allocate data to the correct sub-record within that field. By saying

FIELD 1,(SRN-1)*5 AS DUMMY$,21 AS D$,4 AS N$

we use a dummy field, DUMMY$, to skip over the previous sub-records in the record as the value of SRN (the sub-record number) changes.

```
10 OPEN "R",1,"PARTNO"
20 INPUT "PART NO - 0 TO TERMINATE SEQUENCE ";PN
30 IF PN=0 THEN 140
40 INPUT "DESCRIPTION:";D1$
50 INPUT "NUMBER IN STOCK ";N
60 RN= INT((PN-1000)/5)+1
70 SRN=PN-(RN-1)*5-999
80 FIELD 1,(SRN-1)*25 AS DUMMY$,21 AS D$,4 AS N$
90 GET 1,RN
100 LSET D$=D1$
110 LSET N$=MKS$(N)
120 PUT 1,RN
130 GOTO 20
140 INPUT "PART NO DETAILS REQUIRED - 0 TERMINATES
    SEQUENCE ";PN
150 IF PN=0 THEN 230
160 RN=INT((PN-1000)/5)+1
170 SRN=PN-(RN-1)*5-999
180 GET 1,RN
190 FIELD 1,(SRN-1)*25 AS DUMMY$, 21 AS D$,4 AS N$
200 N=CVS(N$)
210 PRINT N;"IN STOCK OF PART NO:";PN;" - ";D$
220 GOTO 140
230 CLOSE
```

FIGURE 5.4

A run of this program is shown in figure 5.4a.

```
PART NO - 0 TO TERMINATE SEQUENCE ? 1023
DESCRIPTION: ?BOLTS-2BA
NUMBER IN STOCK ? 2000
PART NO - 0 TO TERMINATE SEQUENCE ? 1024
DESCRIPTION: ?BOLTS-4BA
NUMBER IN STOCK ? 2400
PART NO - 0 TO TERMINATE SEQUENCE ? 1025
DESCRIPTION: ?BOLTS-6BA
NUMBER IN STOCK ? 3450
PART NO - 0 TO TERMINATE SEQUENCE ? 2010
DESCRIPTION: ?WASHERS-5mm
NUMBER IN STOCK ? 500
PART NO - 0 TO TERMINATE SEQUENCE ? 2011
DESCRIPTION: ?WASHERS-10mm
NUMBER IN STOCK ? 1450
PART NO - 0 TO TERMINATE SEQUENCE ? 2012
DESCRIPTION: ?WASHERS-15mm
NUMBER IN STOCK ? 200
PART NO - 0 TO TERMINATE SEQUENCE ? 2013
DESCRIPTION: ?WASHERS-20mm
NUMBER IN STOCK ? 1350
PART NO - 0 TO TERMINATE SEQUENCE ? 0
PART NO DETAILS REQUIRED - 0 TERMINATES SEQUENCE ? 1024
  2400 IN STOCK OF PART NO: 1024   - BOLTS-4BA
PART NO DETAILS REQUIRED - 0 TERMINATES SEQUENCE ? 2011
  1450 IN STOCK OF PART NO: 2011   - WASHERS-10mm
PART NO DETAILS REQUIRED - 0 TERMINATES SEQUENCE ? 2010
  500 IN STOCK OF PART NO: 2010   - WASHERS-5mm
PART NO DETAILS REQUIRED - 0 TERMINATES SEQUENCE ? 0
```

FIGURE 5.4a

Practical BASIC Programming

Please write to the address below for a quotation for a 5¼ in. flexidisc containing all the listed programs and files included in the book.

Please give full details of the machine for which the software flexidisc is required.

Publisher for Computer Science
The Macmillan Press Ltd
Houndmills
Basingstoke
Hampshire   RG21 2XS